IN FOCUS

ARGENTINA

A Guide to the People, Politics and Culture

Nick Caistor

The Latin America Bureau is an independent research and publishing organisation. It works to broaden public understanding of issues of human rights and social and economic justice in Latin America and the Caribbean.

First published in the UK in 1996 by Latin America Bureau (Research and Action) Ltd, 1 Amwell Street, London EC1R 1UL

A CIP catalogue record for this book is available from the British Library
ISBN: 1 899365 03 6

Editing: James Ferguson
Cover photograph: Julio Etchart/Reportage
Cover design: Andy Dark
Design: Liz Morrell
Cartography: © Royal Tropical Institute, The Netherlands, and adapted by Andy Dark and Pia
Print: Russell Press, Nottingham NG7 3HJ

Trade distribution in the UK: Central Books, 99 Wallis Road, London E9 5LN
Distribution in North America: Monthly Review Press, 122 West 27th Street, New York, NY 10001

Already published in the *In Focus* series:

Jamaica (1993)
Bolivia (1994)
Venezuela (1994)
Cuba (1995)
Colombia (1996)
Mexico (1996)
Brazil (1996)

CONTENTS

INTRODUCTION

Argentina, it is said, is 'a country with a great future behind it'. This paradox reflects the puzzlement of those commentators who have tried to explain why a country so rich in both natural and human resources seems in this century to have constantly fallen short of its expectations. In the early 1900s, the influx of European immigrants which led to a threefold expansion of the population in fifty years, and wealth based on vast exports of meat and grain, led Argentine optimists to see their country as a hemispheric rival to the US.

By the 1930s these hopes had crumbled. Not only had the wealth from exports failed to generate economic stability, but political life was interrupted for the first of many occasions by the intervention of the armed forces. This cycle of hope and disillusion was repeated with the spectacular rise of Colonel Juan Domingo Perón, his wife Eva, and the Peronist movement. Described as a mixture of Latin American-style populism and fascism, the new political movement seemed to offer more to satisfy the aspirations of the new working classes than the traditional political parties. But this political promise was lost amid authoritarianism, corruption, and a contempt for democratic expression in society.

Despite this, Peronism continued to dominate Argentine life to such an extent that the military or civilian regimes which tried to suppress or ignore it also ended in failure. By the early 1980s, this failure was plain on many levels. The military dictatorship in power had flouted its role as defender of the nation and murdered all those it considered a threat; the greed of those with economic power had led to the dissipation of the country's wealth and the destruction of many of the social conquests which had made Argentina one of the foremost countries in Latin America in terms of health, education or standard of living.

In 1989, Argentines once again turned to Peronism to offer them fresh hope. The new Peronism, as incarnated by President Carlos Saúl Menem, proposed very different solutions to Argentina's economic woes. His government embarked on an ambitious programme to attack the high levels of inflation which had plagued the country's economy for thirty years or more. By selling off the state enterprises which Peronism had originally created, by greatly reducing the state's role in the economy – but also, by throwing historic numbers of people out of work, and creating new poverty and marginalisation – President Menem's government brought a stability which had been unknown in Argentina for many years. In 1995, President

Madonna as the new Evita   (Leonardo Carvallo/AP)

Menem was rewarded with a second term in office. He encouraged Argentines to believe once more that their future could be a glorious one.

In the chapters of this book, we look at how and why the Argentines have so often seen their hopes defrauded, and ask whether the future can ever seem brighter for them than the past.

1   LAND AND PEOPLE: THE PROMISE OF WEALTH

Despite being hopefully baptised the 'land of silver' by the Spaniards when they arrived in the 16th century, Argentina's real wealth has always been the land itself. The eighth largest territory in the world, Argentina has the good fortune to be situated mainly in the temperate zone between the Tropic of Capricorn and 50 degrees south. The huge expanse of flat grasslands which stretch for 2,000 kilometres across the middle of the country, known from their Indian name as *pampas*, are at the heart of these riches. The topsoil of the pampas, created by the erosion of the Andes mountains which make up Argentina's western border, can be up to fifteen metres deep, and is ideal for both cattle raising and for growing many crops.

It was the Spaniards who first introduced cattle and horses to these fertile plains. For many years, both ran free and were made use of in their semi-wild state by indigenous groups and Spanish settlers alike. During Argentina's time as a Spanish colony, the land was largely unexploited. It was only in the 19th century after independence that the pampas began to be divided into large properties known as *estancias*. These were handed out mostly to army officers who had been involved in the 'war of the desert' against the nomadic Indian tribes. With the introduction of refrigerating plants and ships that could transport chilled beef and lamb to Europe, the pampas entered an era of spectacular prosperity. Wheat and other export crops were also developed, and today Argentina is the world's largest exporter of beef and wheat. Other important crops include maize, sorghum, and sunflowers for oil.

In recent years, many of the large estancias have been forced to modernise and to rationalise production in order to stay profitable. There have also been warnings that as the pampas are farmed more intensively, there is a risk of them becoming worked out and the land becoming barren.

Patagonia

The further south one travels in Argentina, the less fertile the land becomes. Below about 40 degrees south lies the huge low plateau of Patagonia, where sheep farming is the most viable enterprise, except in the protected valleys of a province like Río Negro, where apples and other soft fruit are grown. These lands are characterised by constant winds blowing from the Andes in the west and increasingly sparse vegetation, creating a wilderness with its own desolate beauty.

It was also on the Patagonian coast that the first significant discoveries of oil were made in 1907. This led to an important oil industry growing up around the town of Comodoro Rivadavia on the Atlantic coast. Research now suggests that these same geological formations stretch out under the continental shelf, with possible oil-bearing rocks being located within the disputed zone with the United Kingdom around the Malvinas or Falkland islands. The question of who should explore and possibly exploit these fields is inextricably bound up with the two countries' historic dispute over the sovereignty of the islands.

The Falkland/Malvinas Islands

The Falkland or Malvinas islands are two windswept and largely treeless pieces of land, with many smaller outcrops, in the middle of the South Atlantic sea, some 800 kilometres off mainland Argentina and 12,500 kilometres from Britain. Outside the tiny capital, Port Stanley, a cluster of small wooden and tin-roofed houses on the eastern island, the grassy hills support only occasional sheep farms, while the shores are home to thousands of penguins and seals. They have little strategic importance, but the sale of fishing licences and the prospect of extensive oil deposits in the surrounding seas have boosted their economic status.

The islands were possibly first colonised by French settlers from the Breton port of St Malo, which would explain the origin of their name in Spanish. In 1767 sovereignty was claimed by the Spanish crown, which almost led to a war with Britain in 1770. Following independence from Spain in 1810, successive Argentine governments have claimed that all possessions of the Spanish crown automatically transferred to their sovereignty. For their part, the British settled the islands in 1833 and argue that since then they have exercised effective rule over them.

For many years the sovereignty issue was a bone of contention between the two countries. Pressure to reclaim the Malvinas for Argentina increased when the nationalist Peronist government came to power in the late 1940s. Argentina began to press its claim to the islands and other dependencies in the South Atlantic through the decolonisation committee of the United Nations. The British government refused to countenance any change, although the Labour government in the early 1970s appeared willing to be more flexible. Then on 2 April 1982 the military junta in Argentina sent troops to 'recuperate' the islands. They occupied them for just over two months – without violence to the 2,000 inhabitants – until a task force from Britain dislodged them, but only after more than a thousand combatants had died.

The outcome was celebrated as a great victory in Britain, while in Argentina it led to the immediate collapse of the military government. But the futility of the conflict was perhaps best summed up by the Argentinian writer Jorge Luis Borges when he described it as 'two bald men fighting over a

comb'. When Argentina and Britain resumed diplomatic relations in 1990, it was agreed that the sovereignty question would not be allowed to affect relations in other areas.

The British maintained the position that there could be no transfer of sovereignty unless such was the clear desire of the islanders. The Argentines stated that while they regarded the islands as being part of their national territory, they would press their claim only by diplomatic means. Meanwhile, the possibility of significant oil deposits under the seabed in disputed waters between the islands and the mainland has brought cooperation in areas of exploration but has not helped resolve the crucial question of sovereignty.

Navy veterans at a Malvinas ceremony   *(Julio Etchart/Reportage)*

Tierra del Fuego

Off the southern tip of mainland Argentina lies the island of Tierra del Fuego, apparently so called because of the native camp-fires spotted by Spanish sailors crossing through the Straits of Magellan. The eastern half of the island is Argentine territory, the western part belonging to Chile. Argentina boasts the southernmost city in the world at Ushuaia, on the southern side of the island, more than 5,000 kilometres from its most northern town, La Quiaca, on the border with Bolivia. Once again, sheep farming is the main economic activity, although the port of Ushuaia is something of a tourist centre for ships rounding Cape Horn or undertaking excursions to the Antarctic, a substantial part of which Argentina lays claim to.

Ushaia, Tierra del Fuego *(Hilary Bradt/South American Pictures)*

The Andes

Tourism is also one of the main activities in the beautiful area of the southern Andes. Argentina has fewer of the volcanoes which are so characteristic of southern Chile, but it too has its peaks and glaciers, most of which are now part of national parks. Among the most impressive are the glaciers Perito Moreno and El Tronador. Further north in the mountain range are the resort towns where Argentines like to ski in the winter months from July to September, the best known of which is San Carlos de Bariloche. This resort was founded by Swiss immigrants and is famous throughout the country for its Swiss-style chocolate, preserves and other European produce. Less proudly, it was the home for almost fifty years of a former German army captain, Erich Priebke, who is wanted in Italy on suspicion of having ordered the deaths of 335 Italian civilians near Rome in reprisal for the killing of German soldiers.

Still in the Andean region, but further north, on a level with the Chilean capital Santiago, lies the city of Mendoza, at the centre of Argentina's wine region. The altitude, plentiful water from the mountains and settled weather conditions make this an ideal area for wine production. Vines were first planted in the Mendoza region by Spanish missionaries, although it only became a business in the 19th century when Italian and French immigrants settled there. Nowadays, Argentina is the fifth largest wine producer in the world, mostly of robust red table wines. The area around Mendoza, known as the Cuyo, is also important for the production of other Mediterranean fruits and is an important centre for trade with Chile, thanks to road and rail tunnels through the Andes.

North of Mendoza, the peaks of the Andes reach their summit at Mount Aconcagua, which at 6,958 metres is the highest mountain outside the Himalayas. As the Tropic of Capricorn approaches, the land becomes drier and less fertile. This is the poorest corner of Argentina, where life resembles that of the bleak *altiplano* in Bolivia and Peru. It is still common to find herds of goats, adobe huts and isolated communities, some of whom speak the indigenous language Quechua rather than Spanish. Where there is water in the river valleys of Salta and Jujuy provinces, however, the soil is still very fertile, and fruit, maize and peppers are grown. The mountain landscapes here are very different from those in the south of the country, with dry plateaux, salt flats, and gorges dug into highly coloured rocks, where cactus and prickly scrub are the usual vegetation. It is also here that much of Argentina's mineral wealth is to be found, with gold, silver and iron ore all being mined.

To the east of the Andes, the land slopes away towards the huge river systems at the centre of the continent. As it does, the climate becomes hotter until it is subtropical on the borders with Paraguay and Brazil. Argentina shares the low marshlands of the Chaco, much of which is largely uninhabited and unexploited except by small groups of nomadic indigenous people. Where the rainfall has been sufficient to produce forests, the lumber industry is the most important economic activity in the region, particularly for the *quebracho* tree, from which tannin is extracted for use in Argentina's long-established leather industry. Elsewhere, cotton, tea, and the *mate* bush which provides Argentina's local drink, are cultivated.

On the border with Brazil are the spectacular Iguazú falls, with over 275 separate cascades, which offer the major tourist attraction in this area. Tourists also come to visit the ruins of the settlements in Misiones province where Jesuit missionaries tried to convert local tribes to Christianity. The Jesuits formed Indian communities and encouraged them to farm in smallholdings before they were seen as a threat to the centralising power of the Pope and expelled from all of Latin America in 1777.

Hills and Coast

To the north of the pampas, the first hills to break the flat monotonous horizon are those of the province of Córdoba. These are not as high as the Andes, reaching a maximum of around 3,000 metres, and are often green and rounded, cut by many rivers and wooded valleys. This landscape and the existence of quality stone for building attracted Spanish settlers in the 16th century, and the city of Córdoba soon became a thriving centre.

Mar del Plata *(Frank Nowikowski/South American Pictures)*

Argentina's oldest university was founded there in 1621, and its many churches and convents are a reminder that the city was also an important religious centre. In more recent times, the *sierras* of Córdoba have become resorts for those wishing to escape the pressures of Argentine city life – although the city of Córdoba itself is now largely industrial, with many of the country's car factories sited there.

The main cities of Argentina – Rosario, Santa Fé, Buenos Aires and La Plata – are situated on the broad estuary of the Río de la Plata, reflecting the importance of grain, beef and other agricultural exports to the national economy. Almost a third of the country's population lives in greater Buenos Aires, while as a whole, almost 85 per cent of all Argentines are town and city dwellers. As the Río de la Plata estuary meets the Atlantic, Argentina's popular seaside resorts start to spring up. About 400 kilometres from Buenos Aires lies the huge resort of Mar del Plata, where it seems half the inhabitants of Buenos Aires transplant themselves for the summer months. Further south, smaller resorts give way to the wildlife centres of the Valdés peninsula, where visitors can see penguin and sea lion colonies and whales breeding offshore.

Buenos Aires

Arriving by aeroplane in Buenos Aires is an extraordinary experience. Out of one window are the vast muddy red waters of the Río de la Plata estuary. Out of the other, the endless drab green plains of the pampas. Then, suddenly rising out of this nothingness are mile upon mile of tall buildings, a tight cluster of skyscrapers, roads and suburbs that rivals the largest and most modern cities of North America. This impression of size and bustling activity continues on entering the city. With almost twelve million inhabitants, Buenos Aires vibrates with a life and power shared in Latin America only by São Paulo in Brazil or Mexico City.

The Spanish explorer, Juan Díaz de Solís was the first European to land in the area in 1516, but it was another twenty years before Pedro de Mendoza first founded the settlement of Nuestra Señora de Santa María del Buen Aire. This settlement was abandoned after five years and it was only in 1586 that the city was re-established. Under Spanish colonial rule, when all trade with Spain had to be conducted via Lima in Peru, several thousand kilometres to the north, Buenos Aires was only a small port for local trade. The tensions created by this subsidiary position, cheerfully exploited by such 'free-trading' nations as Britain and France, fuelled the desire for independence among the city's inhabitants.

The opportunity to throw off Spanish rule finally came during the Napoleonic Wars. Two British invasion attempts were rebuffed, and then in 1810 the Buenos Aires *cabildo* or council declared its independence from Spain. The years after independence were dominated by the struggle of the city and its traders, looking towards Europe for imports, fashions and ideas, against the provincial *caudillos* or local power brokers who remained closer to the traditions of the Spanish colony and the rest of Latin America. A national constitution was finally adopted in 1853, and by 1880 Buenos Aires was installed as the federal capital of a more or less unified nation.

This and the decision to promote European immigration led to a massive expansion in the city's population between 1880 and 1930. In the early part of the 20th century Buenos Aires was the largest city in Latin America, growing from 750,000 in 1900 to over two million inhabitants by 1930. This figure doubled again in the next twenty years. The population of Buenos Aires came to be known as *porteños*, underlining their identification as inhabitants of the port – Argentina's trading link with the world.

The city's first centre of activity was based around the original fort and council building in the Plaza de Mayo to the south, while the port was on the small Riachuelo river. But an outbreak of yellow fever in 1871 led to the rapid expansion of the city northwards along the shore of the river, and growth since then has been mainly north and west into the flat pampas of Buenos Aires province. In 1880, following the example of Haussmann in Paris, the mayor of Buenos Aires, Torcuato de Alvear, widened the old colonial streets, created broad avenues and began planning the modern infrastructure, which in the 1890s included the first underground railway system in Latin America. Buenos Aires was also the centre of the national railway system, built and owned mainly by the British.

Two kinds of building characterised the capital in the early years of the 20th century. The landowning upper classes lived in heavily ornate French-style town houses, built with elaborate stonework and filled with solidly 'elegant' furniture. At the other end of the scale were the *conventillos* or slum tenements, where the newly-arrived immigrants were lodged. These immigrants had been promised housing, a job and sometimes land by the Argentine government, but all too often found that little of this materialised, so that what were meant to be temporary lodgings in the port areas of the city often became permanent. In 1915, 2,462 of these conventillos were registered, with 140,000 people living in them, at an average of between five and ten per room.

Between these two extremes, the rapidly expanding Buenos Aires became a city of *barrios* or suburbs. These suburbs sprang up as people moved out from the centre or came to the city from the provinces and settled in the area closest to their work or around ethnic communities. As a result, many surprisingly different suburbs now exist side by side; one may be typically Hasidic Jewish, another where Japanese immigrants have settled, another where the English preferred to congregate and set up their clubs and schools.

Unlike Europe, where many cities have been badly mauled in two 20th-century wars, Buenos Aires' architecture reflects a continuity of experience, with buildings from each decade existing alongside each other. There have been periods of urban destruction, especially when military governments bulldozed historic areas to create vast motorways and other 'pharaonic' projects, but much of 19th century Buenos Aires survives today. In the city centre the blocks of flats have grown ever taller, while a number of new focal points for the huge city have become important, such as Flores or Belgrano. At the same time, Buenos Aires has its share of the kind of shanty towns which ring all large Latin American cities. According to figures from the 1991 census, there were 500,000 households in greater Buenos Aires living without the most basic necessities. The vast majority of the inhabitants of these *villas miserias* are immigrants from the interior or from neighbouring countries, brought by the often false promise of work in the Argentine capital.

The First Argentines

It is generally accepted that Argentina was one of the last countries of the Americas to be settled, as it seems likely that the original inhabitants migrated downwards from the north after crossing the Bering Straits from Asia some 25,000 years ago. Before the arrival of the Spaniards, indigenous groups were largely scattered and isolated. Perhaps 50,000 people lived in the north-

Wichí fishing   *(John Palmer/Survival International)*

eastern Chaco region, where the rivers and heavy rainfall allowed them to live from fishing and planting beans and manioc. In Patagonia, there appear to have been communities living close to the seashore, sheltering in caves rather than building their own dwellings. Elsewhere on the plains, there were scattered bands of nomadic hunters, who also left little evidence of large settlements.

It was only in the north-west, in the foothills of the Andes and in the area neighbouring Bolivia that archaeologists have found traces of a more developed civilisation. The indigenous groups who settled there grew maize and made elaborate pottery, and were gradually absorbed into the Tiahuanaco civilisation of Bolivia and then into that of the Incas in Peru. Remains of their fortified settlements can still be visited in places such as Tilcara in the *quebrada* of Humahuaca.

Today, there are many small groups of indigenous people still living in Argentina. Recent estimates put their numbers at about 300,000, or one per cent of the total population. Perhaps the largest concentration is to be found in the Chaco, the great marshlands on the river Pilcomayo in the provinces of Salta, Chaco and Formosa. Here there are said to be 15,000 descendants of the Wichí tribe living from fishing and subsistence farming. The Wichí won an important legal victory in the early 1990s when they succeeded in convincing the local authorities that they were the rightful owners of some 400,000 hectares of land in the province despite having no written documents to prove their title. In spite of this recognition, however, the Wichí have still not been granted the single communal title to the land that they were seeking. This denial of the rights of surviving indigenous groups is common throughout Argentina, as little heed is paid to their contribution to the country's history or development.

The Spanish Colony

Spanish colonisation mostly followed a similar route to that of the first inhabitants. Although Buenos Aires was set up on the Río de la Plata estuary in 1536, the majority of early Spanish settlers came down from Peru, and towns like Salta, Santiago del Estero, or Córdoba in the north, or Mendoza in the west were more important than the settlement on the estuary. The failure to discover precious metals or a thriving native civilisation meant that for many years Argentina remained an undeveloped outpost of the Spanish empire, whose main economic activity was the supply of mules and tallow for Peru and Bolivia. There was no demand in Europe at that time for Argentina's wheat or beef, which were in any case very difficult to export. Until 1776, Argentina was part of the viceroyalty of Peru, which meant that all trade with Spain had to be carried out through Lima, making Argentina the furthest – and hence the most expensive – link in the chain for all goods imported from the metropolis.

As a result, the population of Argentina grew only slowly through the 17th and 18th centuries. By the time of independence in 1810, it was reckoned to be around 360,000, with half of this total accounted for by local indigenous groups. As was the case everywhere else in Latin America, the mixed race or *mestizo* population gradually came to outnumber those born in or directly linked to Spain.

One of the most noteworthy elements in this mixed society were the *gauchos*. These horsemen rounded up and killed the cattle which roamed more or less freely on the pampas after their introduction by the Spaniards in the 16th century, and became a symbol of freedom themselves, working when necessary, but always moving on. As the pampas were gradually fenced off for ranches in the 19th century, the gauchos became absorbed into a more stable economy and lost most of their distinctive way of life.

Martín Fierro

The myth of the freedom-loving gaucho or cowboy of the Argentine pampas – the man who recognised no master, who loved the vast open spaces, his horse and the truth of his own violent emotions above everything else – was enshrined in a popular epic poem, *Martín Fierro*, written by José Hernández in 1872. Hernández takes the form of sung poetry typical of the gauchos, the *payada* or contest between two guitar players who try to outdo each other in verses that are topical, satirical, romantic or erotic, and uses this tradition to lament the passing of an age of greater heroism and liberty. Boasting of his horse-riding skills, Fierro praises the power of the Indians' horses:

Catching rhea with bolas

(Tony Morrison/South American Pictures)

There isn't a danger in all the world,
But mounted well I'll meet;
  The Indian's horse was a glossy black,
I was fit for anything on its back,
It could cover the ground like a leaping hound
with the 'bolas' round its feet.

The poem was immensely popular, and Hernández had to write a sequel, *La vuelta de Martín Fierro* (*The Return of Martín Fierro*), to satisfy demand. It is still recited in Argentine schools, and runs deep in the national character as the romantic ideal of an outsider persecuted by blind, uncomprehending authority.

One element noticeably lacking in Argentina's racial mix is that of black people. In the 18th century, the British supplied African slaves to Argentina as they did elsewhere on the continent, but since Argentina was not a plantation economy most were employed as domestic servants. There is known to have been a black battalion which followed General San Martín in his campaigns to oust the Spaniards from the rest of Latin America, but as the 19th century progressed, traces of this black population gradually disappeared.

Immigrant Nation

Argentina is often seen as the most 'European' of Latin American countries. This is largely because successive governments from the late 1860s onwards have followed the dictum *gobernar es poblar* ('to govern is to populate') and encouraged immigration, particularly from Europe. Those attracted were not only from Spain, but also from Italy and other Mediterranean countries.

Many of these were seasonal agricultural labourers, who worked in harvests in their own countries and came to Argentina to do the same in the southern summer. Because they appeared with the summer months and disappeared for the winter they were known as *golondrinas* or 'swallows'.

The Welsh in Patagonia

Herbert Jones, a thin, alert old man in his eighties, is the gravedigger in the small town of Gaiman in the Chubut valley in Patagonia. He sits surrounded by the Welsh slate gravestones of families such as the Evans, the Williams, and others from the tiny community of 150 which in 1865 set out from Liverpool to escape the persecution of their religion and language by the English, and came ashore at Puerto Madryn on Argentina's Atlantic seabord. They grew wheat and bred sheep, and managed to establish themselves in the valley, where they created small towns such as Trelew and Trevelin. Even today, Welsh tea and soda bread are served in the local shops, and the newspaper *Y Drafod* is still published after more than a century. Elsewhere in Patagonia, the Argentine government, anxious to establish its territorial claims to land disputed with Chile, granted claims to huge tracts, which were also taken up by the Welsh or by Scottish sheep farmers. Nowadays the Welsh have mostly been integrated into mainstream Argentine life, but an annual Eisteddfod or festival is still held in the Chubut valley, and teachers are sent out from Wales to keep the Welsh language alive among the young.

At the turn of the century there were also large numbers who came to Argentina from Germany and Eastern Europe and a considerable Jewish immigrant population fleeing persecution in Russia. This latter group has made Buenos Aires the second largest Jewish city in the Americas. There was also a steady stream of immigrants from the Arab Middle East, who are known as *sirio-libaneses* or, more popularly, *turcos*. President Menem himself is a son of immigrant grocers from Damascus.

President Domingo Faustino Sarmiento, one of the first to encourage large-scale immigration, was also one of the founders of the effective state education system, which has helped to create a strong sense of national identity among the children of all these immigrant groups.

This mixture often seems to have led Argentines to turn their backs on their Latin American neighbours, preferring to measure their aspirations and achievements against Europe or the US, which many thought that they could rival in the early years of the 20th century. Although the writer Jorge Luis Borges said it of Argentina's literary tradition, it is not just as writers that the Argentines consider their country a province of Europe accidentally set thousands of kilometres from the rest of the continent.

At its worst, this attitude has led to racism and a disparaging attitude towards those Argentines born with some indigenous blood, who are known as *cabecitas negras* (black-headed people) and can usually only find menial jobs or work as maids for the middle classes. This sense of superiority often extends to the rest of Latin America as well, based perhaps on the fact that Argentina has not known the huge disparities in wealth and poverty, the racial clashes, or even the high levels of illiteracy that have plagued many other countries on the subcontinent.

Post-War Immigration

One of strangest stories at the end of the Second World War in 1945 was the persistent rumour that Hitler had fled Germany in a U-boat and had made for the Argentine Atlantic resort of Mar del Plata. Although the story proved groundless, there is no doubt that Nazi leaders – Adolf Eichmann and Josef Mengele among them – were allowed into Argentina with official connivance. Documents brought to light when President Menem's government allowed official immigration files to be made public early in the 1990s showed that whereas Germans were usually welcomed, Jewish immigrants from Europe faced a tougher time.

Although European immigration did continue on a large scale after the war, largely from Spain and Italy, this slowed to a trickle by the 1960s. Smaller groups of immigrants fleeing political problems in countries such as Algeria or Korea have been more recent arrivals, but most of those seeking entry into Argentina in the past thirty years have been from its Latin American neighbours. Bolivians, Paraguayans and others have moved to Buenos Aires and other cities in search of work and better prospects.

In the early 1990s, after the collapse of the Communist regimes in Eastern Europe, the Argentine Foreign Minister Guido di Tella sought to revive the idea of Argentina as a haven for skilled labour from Europe. Unlike in the 19th century, however, he seemed to expect the international community to pay for the costs of transferring and training these new arrivals. There is little evidence that this plan has prospered.

With a population of approximately 34 million in the mid-1990s, the years of rapid demographic growth appear to have ended in Argentina. City dwelling, economic instability and the declining influence of the Catholic Church have all led to large families becoming less common. Nor does Argentina have a predominantly youthful population, as is the case with many other Latin American countries.

2   HISTORY AND POLITICS: THE GENERALS RULE

In 1808, Argentines opposed to Spanish rule deposed the viceroy and declared that Buenos Aires would be controlled by a revolutionary council. On 25 May 1810, this council announced Argentina's independence from Spain, although this was not formally recognised for another six years. Argentines under General José de San Martín helped remove Spanish colonial rule from Chile and Peru. In Argentina itself, the shape of the future nation was unclear. General San Martín left the country in dismay in 1824 to live out his life in Boulogne, France, declaring 'to make a revolution is to plough the sea'.

For the next fifty years, there was almost constant struggle between the provinces, which had been dominant under the Spanish, and the rapidly growing port of Buenos Aires. The politicians of Buenos Aires were known as the Unitarians because they sought a unified national constitution, which would give them most power. Against them, the provincial leaders or *caudillos* wanted a more federal arrangement, in order to bolster their own position. Out of this confusion arose the dictatorship of Juan Manuel de Rosas. It was Rosas who set Argentina's precedent for turning to rule by a strong man in times of crisis, even at the cost of personal freedoms.

Self-styled the 'Restorer of the Laws', Rosas ruled from 1835 to 1852. It was under him that the ugly traits of institutionalised dictatorship first appeared in Argentina: the use of secret police and torture; the division of the population into fanatic supporters and those suspected of being disloyal and therefore 'subversive'; attacks on the press and on education. Several thousand people are thought to have been killed by Rosas' thugs, the *masorca*.

Defeated in 1852 by General Urquiza and his Unitarian forces, Rosas chose exile in England, while in Argentina fresh conflict broke out between the provinces and Buenos Aires. The power struggle was finally resolved ten years later, when a federal constitution was adopted. Although Buenos Aires joined the federal state as an equal partner with the provinces, it held all the economic advantages. By the time it became the national capital in 1880, the provincial caudillos had been crushed, largely thanks to two strong national presidents, Bartolomé Mitre (1862-8) and Domingo Faustino Sarmiento (1868-74).

The British in Argentina

After their frustrated attempts at invading Buenos Aires in the early 19th century, the British set about turning Argentina into what Lenin was later to call 'a commercial colony'. From the early days of independence, British banks lent capital to the emerging Argentine institutions, while British industry exported a vast range of manufactured goods. So dominant were British manufacturers that the first British representative in Buenos Aires, Sir Woodbine Parish, wrote of the Argentine gaucho in the 1850s:

> take his whole equipment, examine everything about him – and what is there not of hide that is not British? If his wife has a gown, ten to one it is from Manchester. The camp kettle in which he cooks his food – the common earthenware he eats from – his knife, spoons, bits and the poncho which covers him – are all imported from England.

President Sarmiento and his successors opened up Argentina to European immigration and investment. Relatively few of the immigrants came from Britain, but most of the trade and capital investment in the new infrastructure required by the burgeoning economy originated there. The British built the railways, centring the system on Buenos Aires for export purposes. They ran the gas and electricity companies in the capital. They built and managed most of the meat packing plants and grain silos in the port, as well as running many of the financial services. Despite being small in number, the British had extensive contacts with the local power-brokers, resulting in a strong cultural influence as well, found in everything from schools to sport. In return, Britain was one of the main outlets for Argentina's agricultural exports, and although the British influence declined after the First World War, in the period 1928-30, for example, Britain still took 32.5 per cent of Argentina's exports.

After the Second World War, however, Britain's place as a source of manufactured goods was taken over by the US or by newly-created domestic industry. Since then, British influence, the Falklands War notwithstanding, has largely been symbolic, with the old links viewed as a bygone golden age by conservatives and the upper classes, and as an example of rampant imperialism by the Argentine left.

An English farm in Buenos Aires,1872

The Liberal Republic

The period between 1880 and 1930 was one of enormous change in Argentina. A backward, largely rural country was transformed into a thriving, city-based export economy which took its place in the world and enjoyed considerable prosperity. As the cities grew, so did the middle and working classes. These newcomers on the political scene increasingly found their political aspirations blocked by the traditional parties – which still almost exclusively represented the interests of the large land-owners. A turning point came with the foundation of the Unión Cívica Radical (UCR) or Radical party in 1890. When full (male) and secret voting was introduced in 1916, the Radical leader Hipólito Yrigoyen won office, and until 1930 the Radicals held power. They introduced social security and other measures benefiting labour, kept Argentina out of the First World War and generally pursued liberal policies, which were eventually seen as a threat to more conservative interests in Argentine society. In 1930 a military coup toppled Yrigoyen during his second term as president, and throughout the 1930s and early 1940s Argentina was governed by a shifting coalition of conservatives and breakaway Radicals, who relied on the armed forces rather than electoral legitimacy to keep their hold on power.

The Rise of Perón

At the outbreak of the Second World War, Argentina was a nation divided politically and socially. The armed forces largely supported Italy and Germany and in 1943 intervened directly in politics once more when it seemed that a pro-Allies president was about to be installed. The Minister for War and Secretary for Labour and Social Welfare in the new military government was a young colonel by the name of Juan Domingo Perón. He quickly used his position to forge links with organised labour and became so popular that when the military government jailed him in October 1945, a huge march of workers on the centre of Buenos Aires forced his release.

Perón stood for the presidential elections in 1946 and won a clear majority of 56 per cent. The Peronist movement was born. From the outset its main strength was a combination of labour and nationalist aspirations which appealed to a natural majority among the population, whether first or second generation immigrants in Buenos Aires and the other big cities or people in the provinces who worked as agricultural labourers or in other poorly paid jobs. Perón baptised these supporters the *descamisados* – the ones who took off their shirts to do the dirty work. Peronism invoked a 'third way' between capitalism and socialism, with the emphasis on a corporatist social structure. It encouraged the cult of the leader and to many bore a distinct resemblance to fascism.

Evita Perón with her husband (left)   *(AP)*

Under Perón's charismatic leadership, the government redistributed wealth in Argentina, with a considerable shift in favour of the working class. The doctrine of *justicialismo* (social justice) underpinned the regime, winning Perón firm support among the poor. Other social measures included a minimum wage, automatic adjustments for inflation, paid holidays and pension and social security schemes. Perón's first term in office, which lasted until 1951, was hugely successful. Argentina kept out of the Second World War (it joined in on the Allied side on the very last day of the conflict) and was in a good position to take advantage of the devastation in Europe by selling record amounts of agricultural exports.

Perón used these earnings to finance the growth of national industry, and under his import substitution strategy consumer goods were produced locally. His government also nationalised many foreign interests; in 1948 Perón signed what was claimed to be the largest cheque ever issued in order to buy back the railway system from the British and hand it over to state ownership. The labour unions were harnessed to the Peronist movement and in return were given wide bargaining powers, a leading role in social security and many other benefits.

Alongside him, Perón's second wife, Eva, fought in a highly personal but effective way to improve the position of Argentina's poor. She also promoted women's causes, being instrumental in the introduction of universal suffrage in 1949, and was immensely popular until her early death in 1952.

Evita

Born in 1919 in the village of Los Toldos in Buenos Aires province, one of five illegitimate children, María Eva Duarte left home for Buenos Aires at the age of fifteen, determined to become an actress. Six years later, thanks to a rich patron, she had her own radio show, and in the early 1940s was close to influential military officers. Through them she met Colonel Perón, and they married in October 1945 when he was 49 and she 25. That same month, Evita, as she had come to be known, led the mass protest to get him out of jail, and in the years to follow it was she who proved most charismatic in direct dealings with the masses of descamisados who were the bedrock of support for Peronism.

She created the Social Aid Foundation, which set up hospitals, trained nurses and provided hostels for young women. She also set up the women's wing of the Peronist movement and was instrumental in passing legislation that gave children born like herself to unmarried couples the same rights as children of married parents. This lack of prejudice, her energy and straight talking endeared her to many thousands of Peronist supporters. Many saw her as their instrument of revenge against the upper classes who had always enjoyed the privileges of Argentina's wealth without sharing it; now Evita was the proof that anyone bold enough could rise to the same position. Many among the middle and upper classes regarded her with a mixture of contempt and fear. They saw her as the driving force behind the cult of personality that was one of Peronism's ugly aspects, and accused her of ruthlessly getting rid of anyone who might threaten her position.

Diagnosed as having cancer in 1951, María Eva Duarte died on 26 July 1952. On her tombstone in the Recoleta cemetery was inscribed the now-famous phrase: 'Don't cry for me, Argentina, I remain quite near you.' But even after her death, she was not left in peace. The military who took power in 1955 considered her tomb a potential rallying point for opposition and sent her embalmed body to Europe, first to Germany and then to Italy. After lengthy negotiations, the body was handed back to her husband. When Perón himself died in 1974, Evita's body was brought back from Spain to lie in state alongside him.

The words 'Don't cry for me, Argentina' became one of the most popular songs of the musical *Evita*, composed by Andrew Lloyd Webber and based on the life of Eva Perón. The musical was an immense hit around the world in the late 1970s, but in Argentina it was regarded as almost sacrilegious. 'A total and absolute disgrace' was President Menem's judgment of *Evita*'s treatment of Argentine history. He was even more upset when in 1995, Hollywood decided to make a US$50 million dollar super-production of the musical, with the controversial actress Madonna cast as Eva Perón. Menem immediately promised to make an Argentine version to rival it, but one which this time 'will be a film about the real life of Evita, not one of those fakes that people who know absolutely nothing of Eva Perón's life have been making.'

Perón, recently re-elected, opens Congress *(AP)*

By the time of Evita's death, Perón had been re-elected, having changed the constitution to enable him to stand for a second successive term in office. His second period as president was far more difficult than the first. Exports fell as Europe recovered; state investment proved costly and fuelled inflation; and the political forces opposed to Perón's working-class movement began to organise more effectively and to seek support among their natural allies in the armed forces. The Roman Catholic church also turned against him, while the middle classes grew increasingly antagonistic towards the corruption and nepotism involved in his personalised style of rule and the repression in the universities and attacks on the press. In September 1955, Perón was toppled in the so-called *Revolución Libertadora* or 'liberating revolution' and fled into exile.

The military were determined to rule Argentina without Peronism. Even when they allowed civilians back into power, elections were held which excluded Peronist candidates. President Arturo Frondizi who represented a faction of the Radicals and who managed to win the tacit support of the exiled Perón, pressed on with economic policies based on import substitution and the development of national industry. But neither he nor Arturo Illia, who replaced him after he had been ousted by the army in 1962, had sufficient political strength to face up to the militant Peronist unions on the one hand or the increasingly restive military on the other. The military themselves were split, and the early 1960s was a confused time when different groups in the armed forces vied for power, allowing the politicians to rule only because the generals themselves had no clear idea of how to counteract the continuing influence of Perón.

From his exile in Franco's Spain, Perón played off various trade union and political leaders against each other, giving them inconsistent messages and contradictory promises. He once explained his strategy in the following typically homespun terms:

> When the Chinese want to kill sparrows, they keep them from settling on the trees. They chase them off with poles, not letting them alight, and so leave them breathless, until their hearts finally burst. That is what I do with those who fly too high. I let them fly. Sooner or later they all fall.

Emissaries came and went, reporting back the *líder*'s strategy, but as the years out of power grew longer, Peronism came to mean almost anything to anybody. A younger generation growing up in the 1960s without direct experience of Peronism in power came to see it as the Argentine equivalent of the Cuban revolution, proposing a proud nationalism that was anti-imperialist and non-aligned.

One of the most powerful of these groups was the Montoneros, who took their name from the guerrillas who fought against central authority in the early years of the 19th century. The Montoneros appeared on the scene in 1970, with a philosophy that sought to combine Peronism with radical Catholicism and revolutionary ideals from Cuba. At the opposite end of the Peronist spectrum, elements in the unions and the old Peronist movement were more concerned with regaining power than making a revolution in Argentina, and this tension within the loosely defined movement proved to have tragic consequences after Perón's return to power in 1973.

Meanwhile, military tension came to a head in 1966 and General Juan Carlos Onganía took power. His government was more repressive than previous regimes, as he resolved to get rid of Peronism once and for all. He closed Congress, banned party politics and cracked down on the universities and the press. But Onganía had no coherent strategy beyond repression for governing the country. The union movement, still largely loyal to Perón, became increasingly combative. The first Peronist guerrilla attacks began, notably with the spectacular capture and subsequent murder of a previous military ruler, General Pedro Aramburu. In 1970, other military leaders stepped in and toppled Onganía.

When General Alejandro Lanusse emerged as military president in 1971 he tried another tack. He decided that power ought to return to civilians, and that this time the Peronists should be given a chance to demonstrate whether they were still popular. Elections were organised for March 1973, and Héctor Cámpora the Peronist candidate of the so-called *Frente Justicialista de Liberación* (Justicialist Liberation Front) won almost fifty per cent of the vote, thus confirming the Peronists' claim that despite being kept out of politics for 18 years they still represented by far the largest political force in Argentine society.

Cámpora's presidency had always been intended as a prelude for the return of the 'great leader' himself. But the circumstances of Perón's arrival back in Argentina were symptomatic of the trouble to come. On 20 June 1973 an estimated two million people turned out to welcome him at Ezeiza airport outside Buenos Aires. Before he could even land, shooting started between rival factions of his supporters, with the left-wing Montoneros taking on groups of armed right-wing security guards. Estimates of those killed on what was meant to be Perón's triumphal return vary between 13 and 100, while Perón himself was forced to land at a small military airbase.

This bloody débâcle was typical of the ensuing months during which Perón was elected president for a third time with 62 per cent of the vote. The left-wing Peronists felt that Perón was surrounded by people keeping the truth from him. His government, meanwhile, turned increasingly to repression to control the revolutionary elements within its own ranks. Perón seemed out of touch with a country he had not set foot in for almost two decades, and his health began rapidly to fail. He died aged 78 on 1 July 1974.

After his death, his third wife, María Estela 'Isabelita' Perón, was named president. The political and economic situation worsened still further. Her government was not only ineffectual, but corrupt; the original ideology of Peronism became still further distorted. A variety of guerrilla groups – from Maoist to Peronist – challenged the authority of the state, kidnapping foreign businessmen, attacking police and army posts, proclaiming that Argentina was ripe for revolution. At the other extreme, the right-wing death squads of the *Alianza Argentina Anticomunista* (AAA, Argentine Anti-Communist Alliance), allegedly masterminded by 'Isabelita's' own social welfare minister, José López Rega, created a climate of terror.

The *Proceso* and its 'Dirty War'

By the end of 1975 it was plain that the Peronist government under 'Isabelita' could not last. Its economic policies had failed to control inflation; more seriously, it was seemingly paralysed by the escalating acts of terrorism which blighted daily life in Buenos Aires and other cities. Over Christmas 1975 Argentine television repeatedly showed a publicity 'spot' which portrayed soldiers fighting in jungle territory against a hidden enemy; the references to Vietnam were obvious, although the supposed guerrilla army in the valleys around the northern city of Tucumán was Argentine and very small in number. This television advert was simply one more sign that the ground was being prepared for a military takeover. A senior general declared that 'Isabelita' Perón's government was not worth losing a single life for. The urban guerrillas, mainly drawn from the educated middle classes, continued with their suicide missions, often infiltrated by the intelligence services. In December 1975 the so-called *Ejército Revolucionario del Pueblo* (ERP, People's Revolutionary Army) carried out an attack on an army barracks outside Buenos Aires at Monte Chingolo and at least fifty of them were wiped out.

When the coup came, on 23 March 1976, no-one resisted. 'Isabelita', who reportedly attempted to commit suicide, was flown by helicopter to the winter resort of Bariloche. Most of the leading Peronists, including the then governor of La Rioja province, Carlos Saúl Menem, were arrested, often for their own protection. The guerrillas, particularly the Montoneros, saw the takeover as the removal of the democratic 'figleaf' and presented it as some kind of victory, since it now brought them into direct conflict with the state. What they underestimated was the ferocity with which the Argentine armed forces had decided to combat any threat they faced. Only in the 1990s did it become clear that the military junta led by army General Jorge Rafael Videla, airforce commander Brigadier Orlando R. Agosti and navy Admiral Emilio Massera, had resolved from the outset that the best way to deal with the revolutionary groups was simply to liquidate them.

So began the traumatic period of 'disappearances'. Anyone suspected of guerrilla, trade union or opposition political activity was snatched by armed squads, usually disguised to hide the fact that they were members of the regular armed forces or the police. Those captured were taken to interrogation centres where they were not only interrogated, but routinely tortured in order to get them to provide further information about their colleagues and organisations. In this way at least 9,000 Argentines, most of them young, the vast majority revolutionary in their ideas rather than their actions, were rounded up and killed. There were no trials – only one *habeas corpus* writ was accepted in the years of military rule – and no public authority ever admitted that anybody was being held.

People just vanished into thin air. Families began the long round of influential people who might possibly know what had happened to their relatives, but they were nearly always met with silence and denials. Most of the population went about their normal lives, divided between a sense of powerlessness and fear and the belief that something had to be done to improve the chaotic situation. Many simply assumed that those rounded up must be

A mother holds a picture of her
disappeared son

*(Julio Etchart/
Reportage)*

guilty in some way; *por algo será* ('there must be some reason for it') became a chilling catchphrase of the time. While this horror was going on, the junta leader General Videla could tell *The Times* of London that the Argentine armed forces were acting to defend 'western, Christian civilisation'. Argentine popular magazines organised a campaign against the human rights body, Amnesty International, which was trying to investigate thousands of reports of disappearances, claiming that Argentines were *derechos y humanos* ('upright and human').

Some of the disappeared were shot and buried in common graves. Others, according to armed forces personnel who in the mid-1990s began to admit their part in the 'dirty war', were drugged, taken up in airplanes and dropped into the Río de la Plata. Perhaps the most macabre aspect of these death flights is that they were probably carried out in order to solve the 'problem' before the big international event which placed Argentina in the world spotlight in June-July 1978: the football World Cup. Argentina duly won the Jules Rimet trophy, while Argentines watched the triumph on newly-introduced colour television. Foreign tourists were put up in a host of brand new hotels; and hundreds of young Argentines were murdered in order to ensure that everything passed off smoothly.

There were no heroes in this war. The armed forces violated all codes of respect for law, decency and the rights of individuals which they were supposedly created to protect. Other state institutions, the police, the legal system, and the Church, looked the other way. The revolutionary groups themselves were a poor mixture of contradictory ideas and half-digested theory, imagining that they could overthrow a powerful state machine in a relatively developed country through ill-prepared urban guerrilla tactics. The only group in Argentine society to emerge from these years with any dignity were the Mothers of the Plaza de Mayo, the relatives of the disappeared who marched silently every week around the square in front of the presidential palace, demanding to know what had happened to their loved ones.

The difference between the Argentine military coup and that of General Pinochet in Chile was that no central figure like him emerged, determined to hold on to political power. The original junta stood down in 1980, considering that it had done a good job. In fact, the military rulers were leaving their successors with insurmountable problems. How could they move from a government based on repression to one which had democratic legitimacy? Did they have any forward-looking political or economic vision? A second junta led by General Roberto Viola was quickly swept aside at the end of 1981 by a man who thought he had such a vision: General Leopoldo Fortunato Galtieri.

The Falklands Débâcle

General Galtieri was faced with an escalating crisis. The trade unions were beginning to organise again, pressing for higher wages to keep pace with inflation. Although the military had silenced the voices of opposition, they had developed no long-term strategy of their own for governing the country. So Galtieri made what he thought was a bold, yet not too risky, move to unite the country behind him. On 2 April 1982, he sent Argentine troops to 'recuperate' what the Argentines always refer to as the Malvinas islands. This had always been one of the Peronists' great nationalist claims, and Galtieri was hoping to show that the military were capable of realising some of Argentina's most cherished political ambitions. The General appeared on the balcony of the presidential palace – something that no other military leader had dared to do – and told huge, cheering crowds that this was the happiest day of his life.

It now seems likely that this move was intended as a gesture to force the British hand, and that the Argentine military hoped to withdraw before any fighting took place, perhaps leaving the islands under a United Nations mandate. But General Galtieri had not realised just how opportune his *braggadocio* would be for another leader who was searching for spectacular ways to boost her flagging popularity: Margaret Thatcher. Despite Argentine claims that their military positions on the islands were unassailable, and despite considerable damage done to the British task force by Argentine airforce pilots, the British flag was flying again over the islands by the middle of June. The adventure cost close to 1,000 lives.

The defeat in the Falklands/Malvinas conflict showed that the Argentine armed forces were as ineffectual in military matters as they had been in running the country. There was no prospect of them continuing to govern, and Galtieri was quickly ousted and replaced by General Reynaldo Bignone, whose task was to oversee the return to civilian rule. Elections were called for the end of October 1983.

The Radicals in Power: 1984-9

The elections were decisively won by the Radical Party in its first ever victory over the Peronists in an open contest. The Radical leader, Raúl Alfonsín, was a lawyer who had been one of the few people to speak out against the Malvinas/Falklands escapade. The Peronist party was split and was still distrusted for the chaos of its years in power from 1973 to 1976. Some observers even thought it might disappear altogether now that its historic leader was dead, and because it had always been a loosely structured movement rather than a political party with a coherent doctrine.

Unfortunately, as Alfonsín's government progressed, it seemed that he too lacked a coherent strategy. An austerity plan imposed in order to help pay the ballooning foreign debt was abandoned when it was half-way implemented. Alfonsín's attempts to bring the armed forces to account for their human rights abuses were only partially successful. Following the appearance of a report, *Nunca más* (*Never Again*) on the 9,000 or more disappeared, which detailed the way they had been seized, tortured and killed, there was a great public outcry for those responsible to be brought to justice. Alfonsín temporised, and in the end used the idea of 'due obedience' (the carrying out of orders given by superior officers) to limit the trials to those of the three leaders of each branch of the armed forces involved in the three military juntas.

In December 1985, four of the defendants were acquitted, but the other five were found guilty; the army commander-in-chief General Jorge Videla and navy commander Admiral Eduardo Massera were given life sentences. As pressure persisted for more of those involved to be brought to justice, the armed forces made it plain that they were losing patience. There were attempted uprisings in 1987 and 1988, and although these were easily suppressed by the government and loyal forces, many believed that these uprisings forced Alfonsín to reach agreement with the military not to push for any further prosecutions, instead declaring that Argentina should put a *punto final* or full stop to this grim chapter in its history.

Apart from problems with the armed forces, it was Argentina's economic crisis that proved to be Alfonsín and the Radical Party's downfall. As elections drew closer in 1989, inflation began to soar. The World Bank refused to commit any more money to Argentina, and talks on renegotiating the foreign debt were postponed. In the elections, the Peronist *Partido Justicialista* (Justicialist Party), led by Carlos Saúl Menem, the governor of the small province of La Rioja, won the presidency and a majority in both houses of Congress. This left Alfonsín running a 'lame duck' administration which inspired confidence neither in Argentina nor internationally. The economic situation deteriorated so sharply, with inflation running into hundreds per cent per month and riots breaking out as desperate shoppers tried to buy goods before their prices rose, that Menem was hurriedly sworn in as president five months early in July 1989.

Raúl Alfonsín

(Julio Etchart/ Reportage)

The *Menemato*

This was the first occasion since 1928 that one democratically elected president had handed over to another after free and fair elections. President Menem was elected on an orthodox Peronist platform. He promised the voters a 'revolution in production', and it seemed that he would continue to bolster domestic industry through subsidies and high tariffs in order to safeguard traditional Peronist support in the unions.

Almost as soon as he took office, however, Menem effectively stood old-fashioned Peronism on its head. In order to improve relations with the armed forces, he offered an amnesty to the junta leaders who had been jailed. At the same time, he renewed full diplomatic relations with Britain, which had been suspended since 1982. He also made great efforts to cultivate friendlier relations with the US, which had always been suspicious of Peronism and its anti-imperialist rhetoric. Similarly, the Menem government withdrew Argentina from the non-aligned movement, and emphasised that the country was a natural member of the 'Western alliance'.

It was above all in economic matters that Menem completely changed the direction of Peronism. Far from promoting local industry and state-run concerns, he and his economic team began to dismantle tariff barriers, open up the Argentine economy to international competition and sell off companies

President Menem, 1989 *(Chris Pillitz/Network)*

run by the state for over forty years. The railways, most of the utilities, and even the state-run airlines and oil company were sold off.

The funds raised from these sales were used in a bid to balance government accounts. Especially after 1991, when Domingo Cavallo took over as Economy Minister, government spending was closely controlled as part of a strategy to squeeze the chronic ill of inflation out of the Argentine economy once and for all. The main plank of this policy entailed pegging of the Argentine *peso* to the US dollar, and refusing to print money in order to compensate for any pressure on wages and income that this exchange parity created.

For this bold plan to work, Menem and his minister needed to succeed in several areas. Firstly, they needed to win popular support for austerity measures. They achieved this thanks on the one hand to an immense sense of relief that prices were finally stable after so many years of uncontrolled inflation, and secondly because the Peronists were still able to control the main unions and to persuade them to collaborate. They also needed to boost exports in order to maximise hard currency earnings, and this they largely achieved in 1992 and subsequent years. On top of this, they needed to attract investment from abroad, which they succeeded in doing once it became clear that Menem would stick to the policy and not abandon it when things became difficult, as Alfonsín had done in the mid-1980s.

When he took over the presidency in 1989, Menem was given little chance of success. At first he was widely seen not only as a joke, but as someone who brought bad luck to all around him. Argentina was said to have lost the 1990 football World Cup when he flew out to Italy to support the team. He was pilloried by the Argentine press when he could see nothing wrong with driving around in a red Ferrari sports car he had been given, while calling on the country to accept austerity measures. He spent more time with his friends from showbusiness or football than in political decision-making; it was even rumoured in the press that he had interrupted one cabinet meeting to ask what his ministers thought of the names for the national football team that he had just scribbled down on his notepaper.

Beyond this, there were serious allegations of corruption involving his entourage. Relatives of his wife were accused of trying to smuggle suitcases of dollars through Buenos Aires airport. His stormy relationship with his wife became front page news when she threw him out of the presidential residence; they have since separated. Apart from these picturesque aspects of his presidency, Menem's way of governing awakened deeper fears. He often bypassed Congress to introduce legislation, using presidential decrees more often during his first term in office than any previous president. In 1993-4, he used the Peronist majority in Congress to engineer the passing of a new national constitution, which allowed him to hold power for two consecutive terms. During the election for that second term in early 1995, Menem also offended many people by dismissing revelations by former members of the armed forces about the killing of thousands of people during the 'dirty war' as attempts by his political opponents to stir up trouble.

Nevertheless, in May 1995 President Menem triumphantly won his second term in office, gaining 49 per cent of the vote in the first round of voting, almost 20 per cent more than his nearest rival. This second victory ensured that he would be able to stay in power for a whole decade, as his first presidency was under the rules of the old constitution, and was for six years. President Menem has spoken of Peronism leading a resurgent Argentina into the next century; sceptics point back to how things turned sour for Perón himself in his second term, and predict that history may repeat itself half a century later.

3 ECONOMY: SQUANDERED RICHES

Thousands of cattle pass every day through the huge market of Liniers in Buenos Aires. Their meat is exported to Russia, France, the Netherlands. Huge grain silos line the banks of the Río de la Plata estuary ports at Rosario and Santa Fé, filled with the rich produce of the pampas. In the old colonial city of Córdoba, thousands of workers turn out the latest models of European and US cars. Despite all the upheavals and economic mismanagement of the 20th century (expressed in a typically cynical Argentine saying: 'the economy grows at night, when governments are asleep'), today's Argentina continues to give an impression of abundance and immense potential for growth.

During the Spanish colonial period, Argentina's main commercial activity was the provision of mules and products such as tallow and hides from the many cattle on the *pampas* for the more commercially active countries further north. It was only after independence and the resolution of endemic civil strife by the mid-19th century that Argentina began to export both grain and beef to Europe. Abundant production of foodstuffs has always ensured that within Argentina itself there has been little scarcity of food for the population. Beef has traditionally been so plentiful, for example, that bars in Buenos Aires used to give away steaks free in order to encourage their customers to buy more beer.

The development of refrigeration in ships during the 1870s boosted the export trade. By the outbreak of the First World War in 1914, Argentina provided almost half the world's total beef exports, as well as exporting wheat, maize and other agricultural produce including mutton and wool. For many years the duties on these exports provided the largest part of government revenues. There was little industry beyond small concerns such as tanning or food processing. Nor were the country's mineral resources exploited as in other Latin American countries such as Bolivia and Peru.

Growth of Industry

Argentina's wealth continued to depend on its agricultural exports throughout the 1920s and much of the following decade. However, the growth of the urban working class, based on European immigration, saw the first small-scale ventures in local industry, although these were often not greatly helped by the governments of the day. Yet by the 1940s, industry was for the first time contributing more to GDP than the agricultural sector. This process was speeded up during Perón's first period in office, when both government

Tanning hides for export, 1880s

investment and private capital were used to boost national industry. The first Argentine-made consumer goods – including cars, refrigerators, radios and televisions – began to appear, to take advantage of a market that was expanding thanks to the relatively high wages earned by a large proportion of the population.

At the same time, import tariffs were raised to protect domestic industry, creating an artificial market in which Argentine goods often enjoyed a monopoly. This became one of the most important battlegrounds between the Peronists and the military and conservative governments which replaced them, as the latter sought to bring in foreign goods and investment, whereas the Peronists believed in protecting national industry and stimulating demand by keeping wages high.

The inevitable price of this policy, as seen from the early 1970s, was the chronic problem of inflation. Money was printed to stimulate domestic buying power, with the result that the *peso* was always vulnerable internationally. Local firms were still largely small-scale. They had little incentive to modernise, and if they wished to do so, often found it difficult to obtain foreign currency. Concentrating almost exclusively on supplying the domestic market, they made little effort to export their goods, either in the rest of Latin America or elswehere in the world, so that Argentine exports remained largely confined to agricultural products.

Liberalisation and Debt

The military government which overthrew the Peronists in 1976 immediately began to dismantle the previous government's protectionist policies. The new economics team under José Martínez de Hoz put its faith in the workings of the market, gambling that removing tariffs and subsidies would force the industrial sector to bring itself up to date and to look abroad for export growth. This growth and the control that the repressive military government could exercise over labour could, it was thought, resolve the problem of hyper-inflation which had dogged Argentina for a decade or more.

Under the military, the *peso* became overvalued, and Argentines enjoyed a period of what became known as the *plata dulce* ('sweet money') when everything foreign, from trips to Miami to the latest foreign-made electronic goods, seemed cheap. Foreign investment, drawn to Argentina by its high rates of interest, was mostly short-term and speculative, and did not provide the capital for the necessary transformation of local industry. This meant that the national economy began to accumulate a massive foreign debt. More and more of the budget became swallowed up in debt repayments, so that by the early 1980s, Argentina was the third largest debtor country in Latin America after Mexico and Brazil.

By the time General Galtieri took power in 1981, the military regimes were reduced to taking short-term measures in order simply to try to control inflation and the debt. Argentine industry was in one of its worst-ever crises. It could not sell on the local market, as Argentines preferred to buy foreign imports that were often of better quality and cheaper. Nor could it sell abroad, as the high value of the *peso* priced Argentine goods out of other possible markets. And it could not invest in the future, since much of the available funds had to be spent on keeping debt in check. The only solution the military government could find to avoid the bankruptcy of almost all Argentine industry was to make this private debt public, thus crippling the state still further.

The Austral Plan

This was the disastrous legacy inherited by Raúl Alfonsín's civilian government in 1984. Export earnings, which in any case dropped sharply because of falling world prices for agricultural products in the mid-1980s, were increasingly used to service the foreign debt. State spending was still expanding out of control, while the government was unable either effectively to control wage rises or to improve tax revenues. Spending on social services such as health and education, which for many years had been the pride of Argentina, began to suffer badly. By mid-1985, inflation was running at an annual rate of over 1,000 per cent. Alfonsín turned to an austerity plan and brought in a new currency, the *austral*, whose value he pledged to defend.

LAND AND SEA

The second largest country in South America, Argentina has enormously varied landscapes and climates. Its coastline is more than 2,500 km long, and fishing is an increasingly important economic activity. The port at Buenos Aires has traditionally been the hub of the export economy.

The Perito Moreno glacier in Patagonia is a popular tourist attraction.
(Michel Setbourn/Rapho/Network)

Gaucho horseman crossing the empty expanse of the *pampa*.
(Tony Morrison/South American Pictures)

The port at Buenos Aires, on the Río de la Plata estuary.
(Julio Etchart/Reportage)

Fishing boats at Mar del Plata, 400 km south of Buenos Aires.
(Frank Nowikowski/South American Pictures)

THE BRITISH CONNECTION

The heyday of British influence in Argentina was between the 1850s and the First World War. Although economic involvement has now declined considerably, some vestiges of the British presence still remain, especially in Buenos Aires.

President Menem displays his football skills - a sport introduced by the British and perfected by Argentines.
(Christopher Pillitz/Network)

Vintage British-made bus still running in the capital.
(Nick Caistor)

Lloyds's Bank and an English-style letter box.
(Tony Morrison/South American Pictures)

The British Clock Tower in what used to be Plaza Británica (since the Falkla War renamed Plaza de la Fuerza Aérea).
(Tony Morrison/South American Pictures)

A member of the Anglo-Argentine community play polo in the Palermo Parks, Buenos Aires.
(Julio Etchart/Reportage)

Inevitably, the plan ran into opposition from the Peronist-led trade unions, which were just beginning to recover their strength after the years of military repression. The government had also underestimated the seriousness of the economic crisis and found itself unable to sustain the plan. A second attempt to hold the line in 1987 was equally unsuccessful; the budget deficit grew wider and inflation continued to climb. By the end of the 1980s, it had reached the astonishing figure of 4,000 per cent per annum. In the period after the Radicals had lost the 1989 elections but before President-elect Menem came to office, this catastrophic situation led to violent food riots in several cities. The situation was so chaotic that the new administration was brought in several months early.

Menem and Privatisation

In his election campaign Menem had spoken of a 'productive revolution' and appeared to endorse the two central economic tenets of earlier Peronist governments: using the power of the state to boost and protect national industry and stimulating demand by keeping up wage levels. Yet as soon as he took office it became apparent that his economic strategy would be very different. Reversing traditional Peronist policy, his administration embarked on a massive sell-off of public enterprises with the aim of cutting the budget deficit and reducing the government's vulnerability to further losses. In rapid succession the government disposed of the telephone system, which had lost some US$1.5 billion in 1989; the national airline, Aereolíneas Argentinas; most of the railway network (which had been such a symbol of national pride when Perón bought it from its British owners in 1948); the gas and other utility companies and many other concerns, including the Buenos Aires zoo.

Most of the buyers were foreign companies, often linked to the same few Argentine groups which were big enough to be able to finance the buy-outs. This led to opposition criticism that Argentina's wealth was again being concentrated in a very few hands. There were also frequent allegations that the bidding system for these massive sales was corrupt, and doubts were expressed about the supposedly independent regulatory bodies which were meant to ensure fair prices after privatisation. Yet the sales did significantly help to improve the government's current account position, and in many cases the services benefited greatly from a fresh injection of capital and modernisation.

These measures by themselves were not sufficient to control inflation, however, and it was only when Menem's third Economy Minister, Domingo Cavallo, was appointed that effective action was taken on this front. Cavallo created another new currency, which reverted to the name of the *peso*. The novelty this time was that the *peso* was pegged at parity with the US dollar,

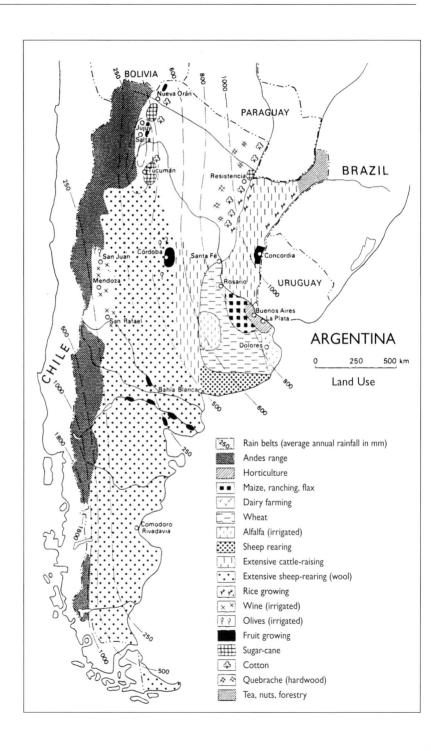

ARGENTINA

0   250   500 km

Land Use

250	Rain belts (average annual rainfall in mm)
	Andes range
	Horticulture
■ ■	Maize, ranching, flax
	Dairy farming
	Wheat
	Alfalfa (irrigated)
	Sheep rearing
	Extensive cattle-raising
	Extensive sheep-rearing (wool)
⅄ ⅄	Rice growing
× ×	Wine (irrigated)
? ?	Olives (irrigated)
	Fruit growing
	Sugar-cane
⌘	Cotton
⚸ ⚸	Quebrache (hardwood)
	Tea, nuts, forestry

with the government pledging that this rate could not be changed without an act of parliament specifically authorising the move. The Central Bank was also forbidden to print any new money that was not backed by foreign currency reserves. From mid-1991, these measures proved extremely effective in bringing levels of inflation down to single digit figures, something unheard of in Argentina for decades. In 1994 and 1995, there were even several months when official figures showed negative inflation. At the same time, economic growth in 1991 and 1992 was nine per cent annually.

The YPF

YPF, or Yacimientos Petrolíferos Fiscales, was the first state-owned oil company in the world, and reportedly the only one which could never make a profit. Despite large reserves of oil onshore and in the seas off the southern coast, the company gradually became a by-word in Argentina for all that was inefficient in state-owned monopolies. Because for many years its production easily covered national consumption, YPF did not actively pursue new discoveries. Because it was a state concern, considered of strategic importance to national interests, no-one looked closely at the books or at the number of people it was employing. Anyone who worked for the company had to belong to a Peronist-run trade union. As it had few rivals in the Argentine marketplace, the company made minimal investments in keeping its machinery or installations up to date. Whatever government was in power, whether Peronist or military, YPF was used as a good way to line the pockets of officials. Inefficiency and corruption were so rife that by the 1980s Argentina was having to import oil.

YPF was a prime target for privatisation when Menem came to power in 1989. But according to Argentine journalists, this privatisation process was also plagued with corruption, and private business interests outweighed any idea of the national good. When finally 80 per cent of YPF's shares were sold off in June 1993, the issue raised over US$3 billion for the government. Two-thirds of this money was used to pay off pensioners and workers made redundant as the workforce was reduced from over 50,000 employees to less than a fifth that number. Even so, oil production increased, and in 1994 the company showed a profit.

By the mid-1990s, the oil industry in Argentina had been revolutionised. Whereas previous governments had seen Argentina's mineral wealth as a resource that the state should exploit in the name of all, now oil was simply another commodity which had to be dealt with as efficiently as possible in the context of the global marketplace. Critics alleged that this simply offered those Argentine and foreign firms with the necessary capital a cheap way to make a killing; the Menem government insisted that, given YPF's past record, the state was better off out of the whole business.

New Economic Trends

Argentina's private-sector companies have been badly squeezed by years of government support for the state sector on the one hand, and cash problems caused by chronic high inflation and political instability on the other. Until recent liberalisation policies opened up the national economy, many private firms were still relatively small, family-owned businesses, relying on sales to the domestic market as they had neither the capacity nor the incentive to export. Few were quoted on the Buenos Aires stock market. Although the list of publicly-quoted companies doubled in the first half of the 1990s, it is still hard for private Argentine firms to raise finance locally, due to a shortage of institutional investors such as insurance companies or private pension funds.

Typically, traditional local firms are being absorbed by large multinational companies. The confectionery company Productos Stani is a good example of this process. Family-owned for three generations, Stani is famous in Argentina for products ranging from bubble-gum to Swiss-style chocolate. Employing some 900 people, it controls about one-third of the Argentine confectionery market and exports about eight per cent of its production. In 1993 the company was bought up for about US$100 million by the international conglomerate Cadbury Schweppes, which announced it would use Stani as a means to export throughout South America. The attraction for Cadbury Schweppes lies in the fact that the average consumption of chocolate and sweets in South America is only one-fifth of that in the competitive European market.

Another sector forced into radical change in the 1990s is agriculture. For many years the large farms or estancias were one of the few areas of the economy to benefit from high inflation and political turmoil. Their export prices were guaranteed by governments keen to collect their revenues on foreign sales; and juggling with the moment to sell agricultural produce or livestock on the market meant that farmers could often take advantage of a rapidly devaluing *peso*. The cost of these practices was a lack of investment in the future, with a failure to modernise or re-equip.

With the economic stability of the 1990s and the withdrawal of tariff protection, a large number of Argentine farmers have faced serious difficulties. Some, especially the larger and more efficient concerns, have been able to take advantage of new possibilities for credit and forward-planning, and this has meant that the agricultural sector is grudgingly supporting a Peronist administration for the first time ever.

The downside of Menem's economic strategy did not take long to appear, however. As state firms were privatised, redundancies soared. Private firms also laid off more people in order to be more competitive. Although exports

ARGENTINA

0 _____ 750 km

Mining and Industry

⚒ Anthracite (coal)
⌂ Natural gas
▲ Crude oil
Fe Iron ore
Sn Tin
Pb Lead
Mn Manganese
w Tungsten
u Uranium
Cu Copper
◢ Hydro-electric station
🏭 Atomic power station
╱ Main oil and gas pipelines
▨ Industrial and population centre
• Main industrial town

rose significantly, they could not keep pace with the huge influx of imports. The current account was only balanced thanks to capital inflows, but much of this money was volatile speculative finance.

The fragility of such investment became painfully apparent after the economic crisis in Mexico at the end of 1994, when massive outflows of capital from that country provoked a hefty devaluation and a deep recession. Argentina just managed to avoid a similar crash, but huge amounts of capital left the country. In 1995 the economy contracted by approximately three per cent after several years of growth. Economy Minister Cavallo succeeded in persuading international investors that Argentina was a different case from Mexico, but the shock led to greater efforts to boost exports and renewed attempts to encourage saving in Argentina – a habit which had been lost over the previous two generations.

Mercosur

Hopes of significantly increasing Argentina's exports are closely bound up with the Mercosur common market. This is a free trade area, linking Argentina with Uruguay, Paraguay and Brazil in a customs union of some two hundred million people. First launched in the Paraguayan capital,

Asunción, in March 1991, by the beginning of 1995 Mercosur became a reality with the abolition of internal tariffs on nearly all goods exported between the four countries. Argentina's trade with Brazil tripled in the 1990s, as Argentine agricultural produce and high-quality industrial goods begin to compete on more equal terms.

Voices opposed to Mercosur blamed it for increasing unemployment, especially in poor regions of Argentina and the other countries, and queried how far either Argentina or Brazil would be willing to restructure key industries such as car-making or sugar production in order to promote harmony within Mercosur. There were also doubts as to how dynamic a market the four countries represented, which made it essential for Mercosur to look for partners outside – to the European Union, or to the North American Free Trade Association – in order to secure future growth.

Unemployment and Poverty

That Menem and Cavallo were able to retain widespread support while they made these sweeping changes was largely due to popular relief at the arrival of stability after many years of hyper-inflation. Even the trade unions, remaining faithful to a version of Peronism which no longer meant protection of jobs and privileges for the official union movement, went along with the government's programme. But by 1995, according to official figures, unemployment in Argentina had risen to over 18 per cent, whereas previously it had averaged less than five per cent. In addition, a similar number were thought to be underemployed, making a total of almost a third of the potential workforce not properly utilised.

Equally disturbing were increasing signs of poverty and even hunger in a country which is one of the world's great exporters of foodstuffs. Social services such as health, education and welfare were cut in line with the government's austerity plans. In response, when he was re-elected in May 1995, Menem immediately promised that he would 'pulverise unemployment' just as he had pulverised inflation during his first presidency. To do this, he spoke of creating 300,000 jobs through public works schemes.

Yet such projects are so clearly opposed to the neo-liberal thrust of the government's economic policies that it would risk accusations of inconsistency and the loss of all-important credibility both at home and abroad. President Menem has spoken proudly of restoring Argentina to its place among the ten richest economies in the world. Many question, however, what consequences his efforts to achieve that goal may have on a large and growing proportion of the Argentine population.

4   SOCIETY: DIFFERENT WORLDS

Juan Farinelli is talking on his mobile phone while he waits for lunch to arrive at La Biela, one of Buenos Aires' smartest restaurants. Diners look out onto the huge *palo borracho* trees in bloom in the square by the wall of La Recoleta cemetery, where all the best Argentine families have their crypts. He sees nothing odd in the fact that the best restaurants are grouped round the cemetery; he has come in a taxi from his office a kilometre away in the financial centre of the capital, where he works as a consultant. His grandfather came over from Italy in the early 1920s, working first on the land, then in a small factory. He had always promised himself he would return to Italy one day, but now still lives in a quiet suburb of Buenos Aires. Juan's father eventually took over the factory, producing work overalls, and insisted that unlike him, his son should stay at school, then go on to one of the new private universities and get his MBA.

Diego Cruz sells the Farinelli overalls in his store in the northern province of Jujuy. Here, 3,000 metres up in the Andes mountains, the air is clear and chill. On one side, the railway line leads still higher up the valley to the border with Bolivia; on the other lies the broad river bed and beyond it the sheer line of rich, red-coloured cliffs. Diego's mother runs the store when she is not planting maize and potatoes on the small strip of land the family cultivates on the far bank of the river. Diego never knew his father, although apparently he was a man from a neighbouring village who worked up in the silver mine run by the Americans on the high plateau. Diego went to the school just up the road until he was twelve, but then could not see the point of staying on. He went to work as a labourer in the sugar harvest down in Tucumán, then eventually got work on the railway. Now most of the jobs there have gone, so he is back in the family store, cutting up cheeses and salami, selling cheap clothes and dispensing strong rum to the miners or those out of work, whose debts he keeps on a slate at the back of the counter. He has never been to Buenos Aires, has never seen the sea, but used to salute the Argentine flag every morning at school, and roars for the national football team whenever he can get the blurred old TV in the bar to function.

These are the two faces of Argentina. One part of the population, based largely in Buenos Aires, considers itself part of the developed world, linked to the global market and living a lifestyle comparable to that of counterparts in Italy, Spain or New York. The other part, living mainly in the provinces of the interior away from the Río de la Plata estuary, has a much more traditional lifestyle. These Argentines are far closer in spirit and outlook to

Urban wealth: Harrods in Buenos Aires
(Tony Morrison/South American Pictures)

their neighbours in Chile, Brazil or Bolivia. The tension between these two elements within Argentine society is a deep-seated one, and one which needs to be properly resolved if the equitable development of the whole country is to be achieved.

It is only with the last two generations, since the mid-20th century, that Argentina has ceased to be an immigrant society and has settled into a more stable structure. Because of the limited possibilities of land ownership in the countryside, this society is highly urban (with 85 per cent of the population living in towns or cities).

Almost a third of the total population lives in Buenos Aires and the greater metropolitan area. It is particularly in the greater Buenos Aires area that one finds the kind of shanty town that is so common throughout Latin America. Many of the shanty-town dwellers are either migrants from the provinces, who have come to the capital in search of work, or immigrants from neighbouring Bolivia or Paraguay, where the standard of living is much lower. It remains true that though poverty has shown a steep increase in Argentina over the past two decades, the average annual per capita income (over US$6,000) still puts Argentina in first place on the subcontinent. Average life expectancy, at just over 72 years, is also very high for the region, and adult literacy is estimated at 95 per cent.

Against this, conditions in some of the poorer provinces of the interior have deteriorated considerably in the last two decades. According to the United Nations Development Programme (UNDP), around ten million Argentines had no access to piped drinking water or sewage systems in 1993. A similar number had problems receiving medical attention, often because they were no

Rural tradition: gauchos
(Frank Nowikowski/South American Pictures)

longer covered by any social security scheme. The decay of the country's public health system, once the most developed in Latin America, is another sad consequence of the political and economic turmoil of the 1970s and 1980s. This breakdown has been accelerated by the Menem government's attempts to cut government spending. Doctors in Buenos Aires' main children's hospital have reported an increase in cases of ill-treatment; AIDS-related diseases are also growing. Cholera and tuberculosis have made their reappearance in Argentina, after years when the country prided itself on their elimination.

Another consequence of the conflict and unrest which have characterised Argentine society over the past fifty years has been the reinforcement of the belief that the individual and the family are the essential reference points. The only people to be trusted are the family and friends; beyond that, everyone is a potential rival or enemy. Any expression of a wider authority on behalf of the state is regarded with great suspicion and often cynicism.

Political Groups

The political landscape in contemporary Argentina reflects this suspicion. Argentines are required by law to vote, but membership of political parties has been constantly declining, and there is little grassroots participation. Peronism, the one mass movement to have emerged in the past half century, is still capable of mobilising massive support, as the May 1995 elections showed. But Peronist ideology has hardly developed in the 1990s, since all the ideas and policies pursued by Menem and his government are orthodox conservative or neo-liberal ones, as championed by the International Monetary Fund and right-wing governments from Britain to the US. Peronism has become little more than a rallying cry to bring out support among the working and lower-middle classes, without any distinctive political content.

Several groups on the left have tried to take advantage of the new conservatism evident in Peronism. The most successful of these has been the FREPASO (*Frente del País Solidario*) movement. FREPASO's presidential candidate, José Octavio Bordón, himself a former Peronist, was Menem's main challenger in the 1995 elections. So far, FREPASO has reflected the disparate origin of its supporters, who range from disaffected Peronists to social-democrats and left-wing groups, and has been unable to articulate a coherent political programme beyond calling for more attention to social concerns and an emphasis on 'decency' in government.

Support for FREPASO and the left-wing *Frente Grande* comes mainly from the educated middle classes in the capital. Their candidates succeeded in defeating Peronists in elections for both houses of the Argentine parliament, but they lack an organisation which would make them effective at a national level. Unless they can achieve this in the next few years, they seem destined to fade in importance.

The small Communist Party is largely irrelevant. In the 1940s, thanks to the impact of European immigrant activists, it played an important role in bringing fresh ideas and debate to the Argentine political scene. But a succession of mistakes, from underestimating the strength of the Peronist movement to supporting the military takeover in 1976, discredited it to such an extent that it was greatly weakened even before the collapse of communist rule in Eastern Europe at the end of the 1980s.

Further to the left, there is little evidence that revolutionary groups command much support. To the dismay of many, some of the former leaders of groups like the Montoneros who challenged the state in the early 1970s and were in large part responsible for the imposition of military dictatorship, now back Menem's government, and even have posts in it. The last spasm of the revolutionary ideal of armed insurrection was as bloody and absurd as the earlier attempts. In 1989 an armed group attacked an army barracks at La Tablada outside Buenos Aires, resulting in the death of 39 guerrillas. Since then, students and other young people seem largely uninterested in political matters.

The dominance of often repressive Peronism or military governments over the last fifty years has made it difficult for democratic parliamentary parties to flourish in Argentine politics. This seems to have been one of the reasons for the failure of the Radical party, when it finally came to power in 1984. It had no convincing strategy for taking the country forward, being forced to deal with the legacy of seven years of military dictatorship and its effects on human rights and the economy. Since losing the 1989 elections, the Radical party has found it even more difficult to put together a convincing alternative for solving Argentina's problems and has been dogged by infighting between rival leaders. After the Radicals' crushing defeat in the presidential and parliamentary elections of 1995, when they came a poor third in the first round of voting, the party plainly needed to rethink its position. The election of a new leader, Rodolfo Terragno, in December 1995 showed that the party recognised the need for change.

On the right, the small conservative parties which represent the interest of the still-powerful landowners as well as some of the larger industrial and business concerns, have found their policies taken over by Menem's Peronists. It was no coincidence, for instance, that Menem first turned to the economists working for one of Argentina's largest firms, Bunge and Born, to form his economic team. Whereas in the 1950s conservatives in Argentine society were staunchly anti-Peronist, they now reserve their criticisms for the corruption they see as endemic to Peronism, while applauding the policies Menem's government is following.

The fringes of the right in Argentine politics are made up of the *carapintadas* or 'painted faces', the military officers and their supporters who staged uprisings against President Alfonsín in the 1980s. They challenged Alfonsín because they felt the government should recognise their role in defending the country against subversion in the mid-1970s and in fulfilling a historic duty in invading the Malvinas/Falkland islands in 1982. Since then, they have formed a political grouping, *Movimiento por la Dignidad y la Independencia* (MODIN, Movement for Dignity and Independence), which seeks to express these views within a legal political framework. During the early 1990s, it seemed as though MODIN's leader, former Colonel Aldo Rico might achieve popularity in this way, but by the 1995 elections support for MODIN had fallen to around one per cent.

The Military

By the mid-1990s Argentina's armed forces seemed finally to have learnt to stay out of politics, not least because they were so discredited after their seven years in power from 1976 to 1983. They failed politically because they had no real manifesto for the country; they failed militarily when they were defeated in the Malvinas/Falklands misadventure; and above all, they failed morally when they indiscriminately used their power to crush political opposition without any concern for legality.

Presidential guard, Buenos Aires *(Julio Etchart/Reportage)*

Civilians demonstrate
opposition to attempted
army coup, 1987

(Julio Etchart/ Reportage)

For many years afterwards, the armed forces steadfastly refused to admit any guilt for their handling of the 'dirty war'. In 1995, however, several people who had been involved in the torture and killing of prisoners in the late 1970s confirmed the methods used. The current army commander-in-chief General Martín Balza apologised on behalf of his institution for the abuses committed during the seven years of military dictatorship, most of which he had personally spent abroad. 'We have to admit our mistakes and do all we can to help the wounds heal, even though we know that this will not be as quickly as we would like,' Balza said. President Menem, who had amnestied the military leaders jailed under the Alfonsín government, was anxious for the matter not to be reopened, stressing instead the current loyalty of the armed forces to the civilian authorities.

Under Menem, the process of trimming military power has accelerated. Numbers have been reduced – there are now only 36 army generals, for example, compared to 70 at the end of the last military government. In 1995 obligatory national conscription was abolished, with the idea of making the armed forces wholly professional. Spending on the military and defence has also steadily decreased during the 1980s and 1990s, so that it now represents only 1.6 per cent of GDP, as compared to 4 per cent when the generals themselves were in power.

As part of its privatisation programme, Menem's government also started to sell off the industries that the military controlled, a huge complex which ironically had been built up under previous Peronist governments in the name of national sovereignty. These included a large petrochemical concern, iron and steelworks as well as the armaments industry. There have also been moves to relocate the armed forces away from the centre of Buenos Aires and other cities. Where before the first army corps had their headquarters in the capital, for instance, a Chilean firm is now building a 'Jumbo' hypermarket.

A new definition of the military's role is also evolving, with the emphasis much more on joining international UN-sponsored peace-keeping efforts.

Argentina has sent peace-keepers to ex-Yugoslavia, Cyprus and Haiti, as well as sending a small force as part of the coalition fighting against Saddam Hussein in the Gulf War. Given the armed forces' involvement in internal Argentine politics over the past sixty years and more, many Argentines are still wary of this new democratic stance. They wonder whether it means anything more than that the policies pursued by the Menem government are precisely those traditionally advocated by the military. It remains to be seen whether a more progressive administration would immediately provoke renewed sabre-rattling.

Trade Unions

Perón co-opted the main trade union movements by persuasion or by force, early on in his career recognising them as one of most important power bases in contemporary Argentine society. Peronism gave considerable power to these tame unions, grouped in the Confederación General del Trabajo (CGT, General Confederation of Labour). They in turn repaid him with their loyalty during his years of exile and have continued to support Menem's very different brand of Peronism in the 1990s. Their power is based on obligatory membership of a union and the fact that social security schemes – and payments – pass through the unions rather than the state as in most other countries. Attempts to change this system in the early 1990s brought the first anti-government protests by these unions.

One of the groups to suffer most from the Menem government's austerity policies has been old-age pensioners, especially those with a fixed pension. In 1992, after the suicide of 29 old people, allegedly in despair at their economic future, the *jubilados* took to the streets to protest. Their actions led to the formation of a new trade union movement, the *Confederación de Trabajadores Argentinos* (CTA, Argentine Workers' Confederation). This new body condemned the CGT as being subservient to the Peronist government, but did not succeed in mobilising great numbers of workers. As in many other countries, trade union power has been checked by the growing number of redundancies and by employers' demands for the 'flexibilisation' of labour. This has had the effect of eroding trade union solidarity and undermining the social gains won by the organised labour movement.

The Church

Although over 90 per cent of Argentines are nominally Roman Catholic, the Church does not play as important a role in society as it does in neighbouring Chile or in other Latin American countries. This is due in part to the relatively strong non-religious state school and university tradition, and also to the strong influence of other groups in society such as the Jewish and Arab communities. Yet Menem, for example, was obliged to become a Roman Catholic as a precondition of becoming president, although this stipulation was removed from the new constitution introduced in 1994. The extent to which the state supports the Catholic Church in Argentina was detailed in a 1993 report, which claimed that US$400 million was paid annually by tax-payers to fund the salaries of bishops and other senior members of the Church hierarchy, to subsidise Catholic universities and schools and to provide grants for seminarians.

The hierarchy of the Church in Argentina has always been conservative. The bishops were strongly opposed to Perón and accused his followers of burning churches in the 1950s. It was their opposition combined with that of the military which eventually brought about his overthrow. More controversial still was the Church's tacit support for the military dictatorship from 1976 to 1983. There were no condemnations of the brutal methods used by the security forces to silence opposition; the Church often gave little help to the relatives of the disappeared in their desperate search for information. Even worse, the report on the disappeared, *Nunca más*, included several testimonies from people held in torture centres which spoke of military chaplains aiding and abetting in torture and other degrading treatment of prisoners.

On the other hand, two bishops died in suspicious circumstances during the violence of those years, and at least fifteen priests working with the poor were among the dead and disappeared. Perhaps the best known case was the killing of two French nuns who were helping the Mothers of the Plaza de Mayo. Belatedly in 1995 the Roman Catholic Church issued a statement conceding that any of its members who took part in the repression 'erred or sinned gravely', but it still refused to make any institutional apology for its role in the 'dirty war'.

This identification of the Roman Catholic Church with the establishment has allowed evangelical churches to make significant inroads in Argentina. Mormons, Baptists, and other evangelical sects look for converts particularly in rural areas and among new arrivals in the big cities. In addition, some young people who have travelled abroad have brought fashionable spiritual movements from the US to Argentina, with a variety of New Age and other cults proliferating, particularly in Buenos Aires.

Human Rights and the Legal System

One of the most significant groups to emerge during the years of military dictatorship were the Mothers of the Plaza de Mayo. These were the mothers, grandmothers and other relatives of the thousands of disappeared, who met each week in the square outside the presidential palace in non-violent protest against the government. They became a symbol of resistance, persisting despite persecution, with several of their own members becoming victims of the repression. Their protests continued even under civilian government, as they demanded that members of the armed forces be brought to account for their criminal actions.

The Mothers were also instrumental in promoting genetic tests on the children of the disappeared, many of whom had been taken away and adopted by military personnel or others who wanted children. The tests were used to prove the real identity of the child, with the aim of restoring him or her to their blood relations. Yet in some cases this knowledge has caused serious problems for the child involved, and has aroused fierce debate as to the rights or wrongs of the move. Almost twenty years after the military dictatorship, human rights groups seem increasingly split between those who are still demanding justice for wrongs committed and those who recognise that the situation has moved on and are seeking to ensure that a dictatorship could never happen again, through education and participation in society.

Beyond these specific human rights concerns, many Argentines agree that a reform of the entire legal system is long overdue. Based on Roman law, nearly all evidence in the country's courts is submitted to a single judge in written form by both sides in a case. In civil cases, this leads to long delays and frustration, which can often provoke violence. In the criminal system, not only are the delays chronic, but the process lends itself to political manipulation and corruption.

Many people accuse the Menem administration of trampling on the independence of the judiciary, first by filling the Supreme Court with political appointees, then by using promotions or other inducements to stifle progress in any potentially damaging cases. Although there have been many accusations of corruption against government officials in recent years, few of these have come to court, and even fewer have reached a conclusion which encourages belief in the system's transparency. Similar doubts are expressed about the police force. Many of its members were involved in the repression of the late 1970s, and torture is reported still to be used to obtain information from criminals.

Social Attitudes

Since the end of military dictatorship, Argentina has been catching up with the developed world in terms of legislation in social affairs. Divorce became legal under the Alfonsín administration, ending an anomalous situation in which thousands of couples had been living together 'illegally'; and in the mid-1980s, many children suddenly found themselves with married parents. Due to opposition from the Catholic Church, however, abortion is still not legal. Nor is there much tolerance of the gay community. Even in the Buenos Aires of the 1990s a homosexual group was prohibited from forming a legal association.

Although a significant number of Argentine women study in higher education and enter the professions, they only account for one-fifth of the national income. They are also under-represented in politics, with fewer than five per cent of local councillors and fifteen per cent of parliamentarians being women. Due to the economic policies promoted by the Menem government, Argentine women have been increasingly forced back into the home, or into part-time work in the informal sector.

Young people are still expected to live at home until marriage, and the increasing uncertainty of job prospects in the 1990s has only served to strengthen this tradition. As elsewhere, the lack of career possibilities and the fact that Argentina no longer offers much promise of social advancement have led to drink and drugs problems among the young as well as a rise in crime in the outer suburbs of the big cities.

Crucially, the state education system which had been one of the country's strongest traditions has been eroded over the past thirty years. Although Argentina prides itself on one of the highest literacy rates in Latin America, the number of children who never reach secondary school has grown steadily in recent years. The effects of high unemployment and increasing poverty have accelerated this process, particularly in the poorer provinces of the interior.

The universities, which had won a great degree of autonomy in the course of the 20th century, were regarded with great suspicion by the 1970s military regimes which saw them as a breeding ground for revolution. Many university lecturers and students filled the lists of the disappeared, and whole faculties were closed down. To counteract their influence, the military governments began to encourage private institutions of higher learning, and this process has accelerated ever since. The Menem government took the process a step further by introducing legislation that for the first time limited the number of places available to students in public universities, and introduced the idea of paying for tuition.

5   CULTURE: A PROVINCE OF EUROPE?

_____ Of all Latin American countries, Argentina is probably the one least attached to its indigenous or Spanish colonial traditions. The indigenous heritage survives mainly in some food dishes and in the ubiquitous habit of drinking *mate*, a bitter aromatic herb which is drunk as an infusion with hot water. The ceremony accompanying mate-drinking, with the passing around of a gourd and the sense of community and friendship that this generates, is one of the few traces left in contemporary Argentina of a different, non-European culture.

The Spanish colonial influence survives to some extent in the Argentine provinces. There is a rich architectural heritage in cities such as Córdoba and Salta. The way of life on the pampas, still devoted to cattle ranching and imbued with gaucho traditions, is also quite different from the cosmopolitan mixture of cultures found in the big cities, especially Buenos Aires. Provincial folklore is expressed in different musical forms: the *chamamé* in Corrientes and Entre Ríos and the *milonga* of the pampas are still a lively presence today, while in the far north, Andean music is also popular.

Civilisation and Barbarism

But from the middle of the 19th century onwards, 'culture' in Argentina has been defined largely in terms of North American and non-Hispanic European models. President Domingo F. Sarmiento was the first to contrast what he termed 'civilisation' and 'barbarism', the former comprised of imported concepts and customs and the latter those of indigenous Argentina or the colonial *criollos*. The rapid influx of European immigrants gave impetus to this idea, which contributes greatly to Argentina's regional uniqueness. Buenos Aires boasts a huge opera and concert hall, the *teatro Colón*, which was shipped in its entirety from Europe. It has symphony orchestras and a large number of performers of European classical music. Buenos Aires also has the largest number of theatres in the region, performing works from the European and North American canon – from Lope de Vega to Andrew Lloyd Webber.

In this century, the writer who most tellingly took up Sarmiento's challenge was the short story writer, Jorge Luis Borges. His writings show an extraordinary knowledge of the European literary tradition from the Anglo-Saxon onwards, illustrating on almost every page his assertion that Argentina is a province of Europe accidentally separated from the rest by a few thousand kilometres of ocean. In other stories, he recalls 19th-century Argentina and the battles which saw the European colonisers gradually establish their dominion over the whole of the country. At the same time, his retreat into fantasy and fable in works such as *Fictions* or *The Aleph* is seen by many as symptomatic of the difficulty of Argentina as a whole in coming to terms with the fact that it is part of South America rather than Europe, grounded in a reality in which the European tradition is only one part of a more complex whole.

Other Argentine writers such as Adolfo Bioy Casares and Julio Cortázar also followed Borges in their exploration of the fantastic in literature; the latter's main novel *Rayuela* (1963), translated as *Hopscotch* (1966), adds a ludic, open-ended fancifulness that has won it success with generations of readers in Argentina and elsewhere. For a writer such as Manuel Puig, most famous internationally for the film version of his novel *Kiss of the Spider Woman* (1976), it was in the cinema or in the interior monologue of daydreams that this fantasy came to life. His books reflect the experience of thousands from the urban lower middle classes, for whom everyday reality meant drudgery and boredom, and who could find escape only in radio or TV soap operas or in dreams of Hollywood. The younger generation of Argentine writers has found it hard to discover a voice that would distinguish it from the perfect fables of Borges or the energetic imaginative invention shown by Cortázar in his best short stories.

Tango

'Argentine tango is a sad thought you can dance to.'
Enrique Santos Discépolo.

Both the musical origins and the precise meaning of the word 'tango' are uncertain. The music itself appears to be a mixture of the milonga performed in the Argentine countryside with influences from southern Spain and possibly the *habaneras* of Cuba. Some believe the term 'tango' to be of Andalucian origin, meaning to play an instrument; others that it comes from Africa via Cuba. Whatever the truth, tango music appears to have first come into existence around the city of Buenos Aires in the 1870s. As such, it was the first urban music on mainland Latin America, and like jazz, that other urban music of the Americas, it was connected in its early days with low life, with the bars and brothels of the rapidly expanding port, where the newly-arrived immigrants went to dance and enjoy themselves. Tango has become inseparable from the idea of a *porteño* mentality, with its feelings of rootlessness and melancholy.

In this first period, tango was almost exclusively music to dance to, without words, and was typically played on piano, violin, guitar and flute. Another instrument which became a fixture of tango orchestras was the *bandoneón*, a key concertina invented by one Heinrich Band of Dusseldorf in 1846 which arrived in Argentina thanks to sailors in the port of Buenos Aires.

The basic steps of the tango dance seem to have been settled from the beginning. It was in the early years of the 20th century that tango first found success internationally, when it was exported back across the Atlantic and became fashionable in Europe and especially in France. Here the dance was divorced from its lowlife origins and was therefore more acceptable among different social classes. As with many Argentine creations, this success abroad gave it increased prestige and popularity back in Argentina, where it was now enthusiastically taken up by the middle and upper classes.

(Julio Etchart/Reportage)

Another important change in tango music took place in the second decade of the century. By tradition, it was with the song *Mi noche triste* (*My Sad Night*), sung by Carlos Gardel in 1915, that tango made the leap from dance music to song. The change coincided with the spread of the phonograph, which helped increase the music's popularity. Of all the tango singers of the 1920s, it was Carlos Gardel who came to personify the spirit of tango both in Argentina and abroad. Born in the French city of Toulouse in 1887 and coming to Buenos Aires as a child from Montevideo in Uruguay, his past was shrouded in mystery. By the mid-1920s he was a star not only of recordings and performances, but went on to establish himself in another new industry, that of the cinema. Together with the songwriter Julio de Caro, Gardel is responsible for many of the songs which are still regarded as the quintessence of tango: *Mi Buenos Aires querido*, (*My Beloved Buenos Aires*); *Volver* (*Going Back*); *El día que me quieras* (*The Day You Love Me*). All these, with their mixture of sensuality and kitsch, their ingrained longing for something never known, can perhaps be explained by a nostalgia for the Europe which the Argentine immigrants had left in hope and no longer felt they could return to, rather than nostalgia for Buenos Aires itself, the tribulations of which were all too present.

Carlos Gardel, with his gentle crooning voice, his trilby, white scarf and perfect gentleman's manners, was the first in a long line of Argentine heroes who have risen from obscurity to win international fame. His position as a national idol was confirmed when on 24 June 1935 he died in a plane crash near the Colombian city of Medellín. After his death, the legend was born, the nostalgic optimism of which was captured in the phrase, *Carlos Gardel... cada día canta mejor* ('Carlos Gardel sings better every day').

Gardel's tomb   *(Nick Caistor)*

In the 1930s tango seemed to become almost obsessively nostalgic and world-weary. As a dance music it had been lively, erotic and frenetic. Now it was used as a vehicle to express the emptiness of Argentina in the years of the Depression, when the country was under military rule, and the hopes of the new immigrant community had been stifled by a reality that did not live up to its promises. The songwriter who most epitomises this urban angst was Enrique Santos Discépolo. Among his most memorable creations was *Cambalache* (*Junkshop*), with its insistence that 'el mundo es y será una porquería ya lo sé ('I know the world always has been and always will be a heap of shit'). In tango the *lunfardo* or working-class porteño slang, said to have been brought to Argentina by immigrants from the Italian port of Genoa, was elevated to the level of poetic expression. As with black slang in jazz and blues, tangos in lunfardo helped to proclaim a specific underdog identity among like-minded people who could understand the lyrics.

The 1940s and 1950s were another golden age for the tango. It was once more popular as a dance; it was heard in every home on radio; and it chimed in with the nationalist culture promoted by Peronism in power. Since the mid-1950s, however, tango has had to struggle to maintain its real popular roots. Younger generations have been increasingly interested in pop and rock music played by foreign groups or their Argentine counterparts, which was closer to their concerns and ideas. Tango became an intellectual pursuit,

Discépolo: 'How I came to write the tango Tonight I'm Going to Get Drunk*'*

'I was in Córdoba at a tuberculosis sanatorium. We'd gone there with a friend who died shortly afterwards. My friend's situation – he knew he was ill, but did nothing to try to fight it because it was useless – filled me with its immense, inescapable pain. In a chalet opposite lived a young couple. They both had tuberculosis, and tried to hide it from each other, to get beyond all feeling, but that too was useless. So then I began to get an idea about alcohol, about *aturdimiento* (befuddlement), not thinking about ills that have no remedy. But I couldn't write a tango about a theme like that, it was too ugly. But the seed was planted in my mind in Córdoba. Then I brought it back to the city, and the city gave it shape. A completely different shape, but with the same inescapable pain. Time, which is as unavoidable as encroaching death. The ruin of a woman who was once young and beautiful is as sad as the sight of declining health. So anyway, against all those things we are powerless to do anything about, I felt the cry of my tango rising: to knock myself senseless.'

among left-wing supporters of Perón, for example, who sought to promote it as a genuine expression of national culture. This was especially true when the Peronists returned to power in 1973. They tried to stipulate that a high proportion of local music should be played on radio and television, and as inflation made foreign imports impossible to acquire, tango enjoyed an artificial resurgence on radio and TV shows.

There have, however, been interesting recent musical developments in the tango form. The most influential of the innovators was Astor Piazzolla, who once said 'I write tango for the head, not for the feet.' Piazzolla was brought up in Brooklyn, and the influence of jazz together with his broader experience of the world led him to explore the way in which tango could be revitalised by jazz rhythms and improvisation. Piazzolla was a controversial figure, partly because he did not get on with the Peronists or the military, because he rejected all the schmaltz surrounding the myth of tango, and because he was often critical of Argentines themselves, accusing them, for example, of 'having the mentality of waiters'. But compositions of his such as *Adiós Nonino*, or *Buenos Aires hora cero* are today considered classics of the genre. When he was on his deathbed in Paris in 1990, all was forgiven, and President Menem sent a plane to bring him home to die.

In the 1990s, tango continues to be enjoyed by many Argentines. Some *cantinas* near the port and in working-class suburbs still play the real thing. Other places put on more refined shows for tourists and produce tango spectaculars 'for export'. There is also a 24-hour radio station devoted exclusively to tango music, and any ride in a Buenos Aires taxi is inevitably accompanied by blaring tango.

Rock Music

Some of the frustrations and discontent of Argentina's young people have found their way into the music of its rock groups, which are perhaps the best known throughout Latin America. The first groups bringing rock music to Argentina date from the mid-1960s, but they first became influential as an expression of dissent towards the end of the military dictatorship in the early 1980s, when groups like León Gieco or Charly García protested about the futility of the Malvinas/Falklands war or the way that young Argentines were stifled by censorship and other restrictions. Another generation of groups has followed on from them, often imitating styles from Britain or the US, but winning enormous popularity among young people, particularly at huge outdoor concerts.

Sport

Apart from tango singers, most of Argentina's popular heroes have been sportsmen, and more recently sportswomen. Tennis star Gabriela Sabatini has joined Guillermo Vilas as a national tennis hero, while the racing drivers Juan Manuel Fangio or Carlos Reutemann are the idols of millions of Argentines. Reutemann in fact used his popularity to launch himself into a successful political career.

Yet it is in the working-class sports of boxing and football that these idols have become something even more fundamental to Argentines. Two examples are the boxer Carlos Monzón and the soccer star Diego Maradona. Carlos Monzón was the paradigm of a poor youngster, beginning life as an orphan and bootblack, getting into scrapes with the police, but managing to use his natural talent and instinct to become the best in the world. Monzón combined the qualities of ferocity and elegance that are perhaps part of the Spanish colonial legacy. He united Argentina behind him when he repeatedly won the world middleweight boxing title during the 1960s and 1970s. He mixed with international film stars such as Alain Delon, and had admiring stories written about him by Julio Cortázar.

It was after Monzón retired undefeated from the ring in 1977 that his problems began. No longer able to channel his violence inside the boxing ring, his behaviour became increasingly uncontrollable. In 1989 he was convicted of the manslaughter of his wife, and was sent to jail for eleven years. In 1995, returning by car to jail after weekend parole, Carlos Monzón went off the road at high speed and was killed.

A similar combination of superb natural talent and an apparent inability to cope with the resulting fame is evident in the career of Argentina's best-known footballer, Diego Maradona. Born in a poor district of Buenos Aires, he never knew his father. By his early teens, he was recognised as a footballing prodigy and was soon playing for the most popular Buenos Aires

team, Boca Juniors. Although he was passed over for the 1978 World Cup, Maradona was regularly the top scorer in Argentine league football.

In 1982 he set out on his international career, moving to Spain and then Italy. But despite helping his team, Naples, to win the Italian championship for the first time in many years, and leading Argentina to another World Cup victory in 1986, his private life seemed increasingly chaotic. Convicted of possessing cocaine, he was banned from playing in Italy and returned to Buenos Aires, where he was again picked up by the police for drug offences. At that point, many commentators believed that Maradona's footballing career was effectively over.

Spectating Maradona involved in *(Daniel Muzio/AP)*
Argentina-Colombia match, Buenos Aires

However, in 1994 the Maradona story took another twist, worthy of the TV soap operas that are standard fare for many Argentines. When it seeemed that the unthinkable might happen and that Argentina might not even reach the final stages of the World Cup in the US, Maradona was brought back into the team, helped them win through and played in his fourth World Cup at the age of 34. Unfortunately, at this point the fairy tale turned sour. In a routine test, Maradona was found to have taken a 'cocktail' of drugs in order to lose weight and boost his performance. He was banned from playing for over a year.

Many Argentines seem convinced that an international plot was hatched to victimise their hero. A novel suggesting that the US World Cup fiasco was a CIA conspiracy, with Maradona being drugged while drinking communion wine, was a bestseller for many months in 1995. In the same year, Maradona returned to play for the team in which he first made his name, Boca Juniors, where he was as much an idol as ever.

With or without Maradona, Argentina remains a nation fanatical about football. Thousands go to watch their team each weekend, with fierce rivalries between fans. For many years Argentine football was strangely free of the kind of hooliganism so often seen in Europe; by the end of the 1980s, however, similar violence was marring games in Argentina, with the *barras bravas* or gangs of hooligans deliberately looking for trouble.

Cinema

The first moving pictures were shown in Argentina in 1896, only a few months after the Lumière brothers had launched the cinema industry in Paris. Since then, Argentina has had a strong tradition of film-making. This reached its peak early in the 1940s, when fifty films were produced each year, from tango musicals and urban comedies of manners to folkloric dramas such as Mario Soffici's 1943 *Tres hombres del río* (*Three Men of the River*). After the Second World War, US dominance of the international industry combined with manipulation of the national cinema industry by the Peronists to produce a falling-off in the quality and quantity of films made. In the 1950s, however, the director Leopoldo Torre Nilsson filmed two excellent pictures, *La casa del ángel* (*House of the Angel*, 1957) and *La caída* (*The Fall*, 1959) which won international acclaim. As the political situation deteriorated once more in the second half of the 1960s, Argentine cinema became increasingly militant. In Rosario, the film-maker Fernando Birri had already made short documentaries such as *Tire dié* (*Throw Us a Dime*, 1958) and *Los inundados* (*Flooded Out*, 1961); his example was followed in the 'new Latin American cinema movement' by the directors Fernando Solanas and Octavio Getino. Their social protest film *La hora de los hornos* (*The Hour of the Furnaces*, 1968) launched the idea of film as revolutionary polemic, not to be shown as entertainment but as a spur to debate and action.

This idea of cinema as social agitation was anathema to the military governments which ruled after 1976, and many film-makers were driven abroad. Those who stayed were subjected to demeaning and often irrational censorship decisions, which made these lean years for the Argentine film industry. It was only with the advent of Alfonsín's civilian government that this situation was reversed, and for several years cinema-making enjoyed a new boom. In 1985 Argentina won its first Oscar, for the film *La historia oficial* (*Official Version*) directed by Luis Puenzo, a dramatic investigation into the lies told and accepted during the military dictatorship. Another Argentine film-maker who won international plaudits was María Luisa Bemberg, whose 1980s films *Camila* and *Miss Mary* were both popular and critical successes.

In 1986, the levels of production in Argentine cinema were almost back up to those of the early 1940s, but unfortunately the economic crisis which brought about the downfall of Alfonsin's government also made it extremely difficult for national films to recoup their costs, and the heady days of the mid-1980s soon became little more than a memory. By the time that economic stability returned, the number of cinemas was calculated to have shrunk from more than 3,000 to under 300, with a box office success being measured in hundreds of thousands of dollars rather than in millions. Production has dwindled accordingly, with only half a dozens films now being made each year.

The Media

The Argentine media have faced many difficulties over the past fifty years. General Perón and Evita were quick to realise the importance of harnessing the media to create a positive image of their regime, and they took control of both radio and the press. The Peronists closed down the daily newspaper, *La Prensa*, and censored other publications. In many ways, this pattern of government interference – on the one hand, the buying of journalists to ensure their support, on the other suppressing any 'negative' reporting – continued under the governments which supplanted Peronism.

Censorship was at its most severe during the military government between 1976 and 1983. Journalists suspected of sympathising with any of the guerrilla groups joined the lists of the 'disappeared'; many others were driven into exile. No reporting of human rights abuses was tolerated; once again, a disquieting aspect of the repression was the willingness of much of the media to go along with it.

Happily, since the reimposition of civilian rule the Argentine press seems to have regained much of its vigour. In spite of occasional tension with the authorities, journalists regularly publish stories exposing government corruption and undemocratic practices. There are over a dozen daily newspapers in Buenos Aires, ranging from *Clarín*, with a circulation of over half a million copies, to the English-language *Buenos Aires Herald*, which sells some 20,000 copies. There is also a strong tradition of regional journalism, with daily newspapers based in most of the provincial capitals.

Argentine television, most of which is now in private hands, is neither better nor worse than that of most other Latin American countries, relying as it does on a diet of soap operas, game shows and sensationalist news stories.

WHERE TO GO, WHAT TO SEE

Any visitor to Argentina will need to take into account its sheer size as well as the very varied weather conditions depending on the time of year. During the summer months from December to the end of February, the southern mountains and Patagonia are ideal for camping and walking; in the winter, the mountains are the place to go to ski. The summer months in the north-east are usually scorchingly hot, while Buenos Aires can seem something of a ghost town, as everyone who can heads for the beaches.

Another decision is how much time to spend in Buenos Aires itself. The capital has most of the country's cultural attractions, and while it does not have the the range of sights and experiences offered by more historic cities, there are many places worth visiting. A further complication for the tourist is that the *pampas* outside Buenos Aires offer little in the way of spectacle for several hundred kilometres in any direction. This means that the best way of travelling outside the capital is by aeroplane. The largest airline, Aerolíneas Argentinas, offers special passes at low rates for anyone buying tickets in Europe or North America, which allow travellers to visit a number of provincial centres in a month.

But any trip to Argentina should begin and end in Buenos Aires. Most of the hotels are situated in the downtown city area, which is best seen on foot. One circuit could include the historic centre of the city in the Plaza de Mayo, where the presidential palace, the cathedral and the town hall in which the 1810 May Revolution against Spain was proclaimed, are all of interest. The pedestrian street, Calle Florida, is close by, and merits a leisurely stroll at least to window-shop. It is a sign of the times that the formerly elegant department store of Harrod's is now closed, whereas nearby the newly restored shopping mall of Galerías Pacífico, is usually thronged with visitors. This is a good place to buy the typical sweets made of sweet caramel (*dulce de leche*) and chocolate known as *alfajores*. There are also many shops offering traditional Argentine leather goods and handicrafts from the pampas or the north of Argentina.

This is also the part of town for private art galleries, which frequently put on interesting exhibitions of modern Argentine art. At the northern end of the Calle Florida is the Plaza San Martín. It is worth spending some time in this well-wooded square, to observe porteño families chatting or taking their children to play on the swings. The foreign ministry in one corner of the square is a heavily French-influenced building, a reminder of an elegance that unfortunately has mostly disappeared from the city.

Colón theatre, Buenos Aires   *(Julio Etchart/Reportage)*

The Plaza San Martín – whose elevation marks the old line of cliffs that used to form the shoreline of the Río de la Plata – also provides a vantage point out over the docks to the river, with at the bottom both the monument to all those Argentines who died in the Falklands/Malvinas war in 1982, and the tower presented by the British to commemorate the centenary of Argentina's independence in 1910. Some of the old port here has been redeveloped in recent years: Puerto Maderos is another place for shopping, smart restaurants and night-clubs.

Another area of the city that repays a walk is the Boca. This is the neighbourhood where many of the Italian immigrants first settled, down by the docks at the edge of the Riachuelo. This, the original river of Buenos Aires, is now black and polluted, but the nearby Caminito has attractive wooden houses and cafes. Also in the Boca is the Bonbonera (The Box of Sweets), the football stadium of the local club, Boca Juniors. A trip to the stadium on a Sunday afternoon is a good introduction to the Argentine passion for football, especially if Diego Maradona is playing. Other sporting events that are well worth a visit in Buenos Aires are the games of polo or the unique Argentine version of it known as *pato* (the Spanish word for 'duck', suggesting what was originally used for the ball) and the horseracing at the track at San Isidro.

The museums of Buenos Aires are largely a disappointment. Argentina's indigenous cultures did not produce the works in gold or silver that adorn displays further north in the continent; nor was the colonial tradition

Iguazú falls (Tony Morrison/South American Pictures)

particularly strong. The Museum of Modern Art reflects a time earlier in the 20th century when wealthy Argentines could afford to buy art in Europe, but has few real masterpieces. It is said that when a Toulouse Lautrec was stolen from the gallery in 1995, nobody noticed it had gone for several days. Most interesting exhibitions are in the smaller private galleries.

Buenos Aires does, however, have a lively and varied nightlife. This ranges from performances of opera, classical music and ballet at the *teatro Colón* to tango in neighbourhood cantinas. In between, there are many theatres with a broad repertoire of plays, more cinemas than most European cities, and any number of restaurants. Although Argentine food is heavily meat-based, there is also a strong tradition of Italian food. Argentines claim that their pizzas are better than any you can find back in the old country, for example, and there are good restaurants from many other national cuisines. The central downtown avenues have a twenty-four hour a day life, with younger people taking over in the early hours after their parents are safely home in bed. Buenos Aires is a city of cafés, where customers can sit outside and keep abreast of porteño fashion and elegant street life.

At the weekends, a visitor can follow the example of many inhabitants of Buenos Aires, and try to get out of the city. Those with the time and the money cross the Río de la Plata to visit Uruguay. They may descend on the small coastal town of Colonia, go to the capital Montevideo, or do the fashionable thing and fly to Punta del Este, where the estuary of the river comes out into the open Atlantic, and where there are miles of clean beaches.

Those looking for something less grand often go to a country club on Sunday, where families have their barbecues and play sport and socialise. One spot well worth seeing is Tigre, the town at the delta of the Paraná river. Here again there are many social clubs and also houses and boats to rent for the weekend.

The weekend could also be the time to visit the pampa around Buenos Aires. Some estancias or ranches now welcome visitors; otherwise a town such as San Antonio de Areco has a gaucho museum and working farms that can be visited. One of the most interesting events on the pampas are the local rodeos, but it takes either great luck or good local contacts to discover when and where these are being held.

After Buenos Aires, the most popular attraction in Argentina are the Iguazú falls on the border with Brazil. There are about 270 individual waterfalls which fall over 60 metres in the middle of thick forest, and take over a day to see properly. A trip up to this northeastern corner of the country could also be combined with a visit to the Jesuit ruins in Misiones, with perhaps a stopover in the old colonial city of Córdoba.

Also in the north, but this time in the northwestern Andes region, are the provinces of Salta and Jujuy. Here it is the mountain landscapes which are spectacular. A trip through the Valles Calchaquíes in Salta, taking in the small town of Cafayate and its vineyards, reveals a different, more traditional side to Argentina. In Jujuy, the valley of the gorge or *quebrada* of Humahuaca also provides glimpses of a way of life more akin to that of the *altiplano* of Bolivia and Peru than that of the rest of Argentina. It is especially interesting to travel here during the carnival week at the end of February or the beginning of March, when there are noisy and usually drunken celebrations.

Further south, the Andes are attractions for climbers and, in the winter months, for skiers. The two main ski centres are at Las Leñas near the city of Mendoza, and Bariloche, near the lake region of southern Argentina. The national parks here provide facilities from which to explore the many lakes, glaciers and mountains which offer some of the most spectacular scenery in Latin America.

On the other side of the country, the Atlantic seaboard also offers a variety of attractions. The wildlife on the Valdés peninsula attracts many visitors, especially when the whales are breeding offshore. And further north, the seaside resorts from Mar del Plata to Pinamar all have their different character, some of them catering to families, others full of students and young people for the summer months.

Throughout Argentina, the roads are better, and facilities are more developed than in much of the rest of Latin America. But it is still possible, above all in the mountain areas of the south, to find places that are completely wild and unspoilt.

FURTHER READING AND ADDRESSES

FURTHER READING

Brysk, A., *The Politics of Human Rights in Argentina: Protest, Change and Democratization*, Stanford, 1994.
Burns, J., *The Land that Lost its Heroes: The Falklands, the Post-War and Alfonsín*, London, 1987.
Charlton, M., *The Little Platoon*, Oxford, 1989.
Collier, S. *et al*, *Tango!*, London, 1996.
Crassweller, R.D., *Perón and the Enigmas of Argentina*, New York, 1987.
Fisher, J., *Mothers of the Disappeared*, London, 1989.
Fisher, J., *Out of the Shadows: Women Resistance and Politics in South America*, London, 1993.
Freedman, L. and Gamba-Stonehouse, V., *Signals of War*, London, 1990.
Gerruti, G. and Ciancaglini, S., *El octavo círculo*, Buenos Aires, 1991.
Gillespie, R., *Soldiers of Perón*, Oxford, 1982.
Graham-Yooll, A., *A State of Fear: Memories of Argentina's Nightmare*, London, 1986.
Hennessy, A. and King, J., *The Land that England Lost: Argentina and Britain, a Special Relationship*, London, 1992.
Manzetti, L., *Institutions, Parties and Coalitions in Argentine Politics*, Pittsburgh, 1993.
Martínez, T.E., *Santa Evita*, Buenos Aires, 1995.
Naipaul, V.S., *The Return of Eva Perón*, London, 1980.
Partnoy, A., *The Little School: Tales of Disappearance and Survival in Argentina*, London, 1988.
Rock, D., *Argentina, 1516-1987*, Berkeley, 1987.
Rock, D., *Authoritarian Argentina*, Berkeley, 1993.
Terragno, Rodolfo, *The Challenge of Real Development: Argentina in the 21st Century*, Boulder CO, 1988.
Verbitsky, H., *Robo para la corona: los frutos prohibidos del árbol de la corrupción*, Buenos Aires, 1991.

FICTION

Bioy Casares, A., *The Dream of the Hero*, London, 1987.
Borges, J.L., *Fictions*, London, 1965.
Cortázar, J., *Hopscotch*, New York, 1966.
Puig, M., *Kiss of the Spider Woman*, London, 1979.
Valenzuela, L., *The Lizard's Tail*, London, 1987.

ADDRESSES

Argentine Embassy,
53 Hans Place,
London SW1X 0LA
Tel: 0171-584-6494

Argentine Consulate,
100 Brompton Road,
London SW3 1ER
Tel: 0171-589-3104
(Tourism information and enquiries)

Argentina Tourist Service,
47 Causton Street,
London SW1P 4AT
Tel: 0171-976-5511

Argentina Tours & Travel,
120 Wilton Street,
London SW1V 1JZ
Tel: 0171-233-5384

Journey Latin America,
14-16 Devonshire Road,
London W4 2HD

FACTS AND FIGURES

A GEOGRAPHY

Official name: República de Argentina

Situation: in southern South America, between 22° and 55° N and 55° and 73° W. Bordered by Uruguay, Brazil, Paraguay, Bolivia and Chile, Argentina stretches 3,460 kilometres from north to south, and at reaches 1,580 kilometres at its widest point.

Surface area: 2,766,889 sq km (almost 30% the size of Europe). This area does not include the Malvinas or Falklands Islands, nor the Antarctic territory Argentina claims.

Administrative division: Argentina is a federal republic, with one federal district (Buenos Aires) and 23 provinces (including Tierra del Fuego). Federal capital; Buenos Aires: 2,900,794 (1991); over 11 million in greater Buenos Aires area.

Other main cities (1990 estimates): Córdoba 1.2 million; Rosario 1.1 million; Mendoza 750,000; La Plata 650,000; San Miguel de Tucumán 630,000; Mar del Plata 520,000; San Juan 360,000; Salta 340,000; Santa Fe 340,000; Resistencia 300,000; Bahía Blanca 260,000.

Infrastructure: there are over 210,000 kilometres of roads linking all the main population centres, although less than a

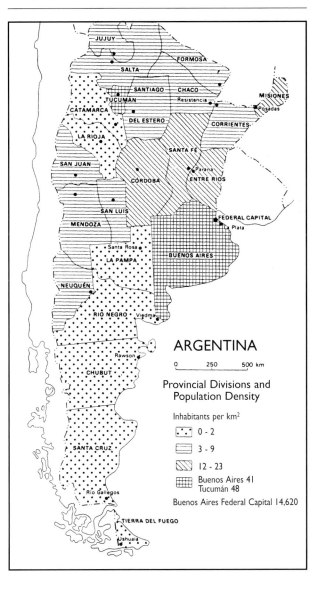

ARGENTINA

0   250   500 km

Provincial Divisions and Population Density

Inhabitants per km²

- ⬚ 0 - 2
- ⬚ 3 - 9
- ⬚ 12 - 23
- ⬚ Buenos Aires 41
  Tucumán 48

Buenos Aires Federal Capital 14,620

third of these are paved. These include the Panamerican highway, which runs from the north to the south of the country. Most of the major roads converge on the capital. The railway system, once the most extensive in South America, has contracted substantially in the 1990s. In 1987 the total rail network was almost 35,000 kilometres; less than half of this is now operating. Buenos Aires has an underground railway system comprising five lines, which has now been privatised. Ambitious expansion plans have yet to be finalised. Buenos Aires has two airports: the main international airport at Ezeiza, and a smaller local one at Aeroparque Jorge Newbery. In 1995, a scheme was launched to build a third major aiport on an artificial island in the Río de la Plata. There are another eight international airports in the provinces; most provincial capitals have an airport. The national airline, Aerolíneas Argentinas, was sold to Iberia of Spain in 1992. In 1995, Iberia attempted to sell most of its shareholdings in the company. Domestic flights are provided by Austral and a new company, Líneas Aéreas Privadas Argentinas. The country's main ports are Buenos Aires, La Plata, Rosario, Santa Fe and Bahía Blanca. The main shipping firm is Empresas Líneas Marítimas Argentinas.

Relief and landscape: Argentina's regions can be divided into four distinct geographic areas: the Andean region; Mesopotamia and the north-east; the *pampas*; and Patagonia. The Andean region covers the whole country from north to south, lower in Tierra del Fuego and the south, with many glaciers; higher and drier in the north, with the highest peak in South America at Aconcagua (6,958 metres). Mesopotamia and the north-east of Argentina are dominated by the plains of the Chaco and the river system of the rivers Paraná and Uruguay. These plains cover some 580,000 square kilometres. The *pampas* form a broad swathe across Argentina's heartlands. The western part, receiving less rain, is known as the Dry Pampa; to the east is the wetter, more productive Humid Pampa. Altogether, the *pampas* cover some 650,000 square kilometres. To the south of the *pampas*, much less densely populated, lies Patagonia, mainly given over to extensive farming. Its area is approximately 780,000 kilometres. Off the mainland lies Tierra del Fuego, which is cold, wet and mountainous. Argentina also has an Atlantic coastline of over 2,500 kilometres.

Temperature and rainfall: because of its size and geographical location, Argentina experiences a wide range of climate. In the north, the climate is subtropical, with temperatures over 40°C in the summer months between December and February. In the *pampas* region, where most of the population lives, it is temperate, although in Buenos Aires summer temperatures frequently reach 35°C with very high humidity. In Patagonia, the temperatures are rarely above 20°C, with fierce winds. The southern Andes receive plentiful snow; the skiing season stretches from June to the end of August.

Flora and fauna: Argentina's varied regions support a wide range of animal and plant life. The southern Atlantic off Argentina's coasts is home to killer and southern right whales; seals, sea lions and penguins also flourish. The *pampas* are known for their *guanacos*, the South American ostrich or *rhea*, armadillos and many types of rodent. Bird life is particularly varied in the *pampas*, with flamingoes, egrets, spoonbills and *horneros* (oven birds) which build mud nests on telegraph poles. The Andean region still has many condors and other large birds; the mountain forests are home to wildcats and pumas. Mesopotamia has a subtropical fauna, with parakeets and monkeys still common; where there is sufficient rainfall, lush vegetation abounds.

B   POPULATION

Population: 32,608,560 (1991 census).
Population growth: (1980-1985) 1.4%; (1990-1995) 1.2%.
Population density: 12 inhabitants per sq km.
Urbanisation: 85%.
Age structure: (0-14): 13%; (15-59): 57%; (60+): 30%.
Fertility rate: (1990-1995 average): 2.9%.
Birthrate: 2.1% (1990)
Mortality rate: 0.9% (1990)
Infant mortality: 29 per 1,000 live births (1992).
Average life expectancy: males 68, females 75 (1992).
Population per doctor: 330 (1992)

Per capita calorie consumption: 3,070 (130% of requirement).
Adult literacy rate: (1992) 96%.
Education: education from pre-school to university level is free-of-charge and is officially compulsory between the ages of 6 and 14. Secondary education lasts between 4 and 6 years, usually leading to the *bachillerato* or normal certificate of education. Non-university higher education or vocational courses last 3 or 4 years, while university degree courses take 4 years or more. Total enrolment in the late 1980s was equivalent to 96% of children of school age but high drop-out rates have been reported, especially in remote rural areas.

Universities: there are 29 state universities and 23 private universities; funding for the state universities has been drastically reduced in recent years.
Social Development Index (UNDP Human Development Index 1994): 30th position out of a total of 174.
Ethnic composition: 85% European; 15% *mestizo* (mixed European-Indian descent). There is a small indigenous population of approximately 300,000 or 1% of the total population.
Language: Spanish; small percentage of indigenous languages in north and east.

C   HISTORY AND POLITICS

Some key dates: * 1516: Juan Díaz de Solís explores Río de la Plata estuary * 1536: first foundation of Buenos Aires by Pedro de Mendoza; settlement destroyed by indigenous groups * 1580: second foundation of Buenos Aires by Juan de Garay * 1778: birth of José de San Martín * 1806-7: unsuccessful attempts by British army to take Buenos Aires * 1810: Buenos Aires *cabildo* or revolutionary council declares freedom from Spain * 1816: formal declaration of Argentine independence * 1817-9: San Martín fights for independence in Chile and Peru * 1835-52: rule by military *caudillo* Juan

Manuel de Rosas * 1853-61: first unified national constitution followed by struggle between federalists (provinces) and unitarians (Buenos Aires) * 1868-1874: Domingo F. Sarmiento president * 1880: Buenos Aires replaces Rosario as national capital * 1890: founding of Unión Cívica Radical or Radical party * 1916: first universal male suffrage; Radical party's Hipólito Yrigoyen elected president * 1930: Yrigoyen deposed by military; start of period of military rule known as the 'infamous decade' * 1943: national revolution led by nationalist military officers,

among them Colonel Juan Domingo Perón * 1945: Perón arrested, freed after massive popular protest * 1946: Perón elected president for first term * 1951: Perón's second term as president * 1952: Eva Duarte de Perón dies of cancer * 1955: Perón ousted in military coup known as 'liberating revolution' * 1960s: struggle for power between different military factions * 1966: General Juan Carlos Onganía comes to power; Congress closed; repression against Peronist and other political parties increased * 1970: Onganía ousted by fellow officers; General Alejandro Lanusse eventually takes over as president * 1973: Peronists allowed to stand in elections; their candidate, Héctor Cámpora wins * 1973: fresh elections; Perón, elected president for the third time, dies a few months later, leaving his widow Estela 'Isabelita' as president * 1976: military coup as violence and political chaos increase * 1976-1983: period of the *proceso militar*; over 9,000 people 'disappear' at the hands of the authorities * 1982: junta leader General Leopoldo Fortunato Galtieri sends troops in April to 'recuperate' Falklands/Malvinas islands; British task force retakes them by mid-June * 1983-84: collapse of military regime; Radical party leader Raúl Alfonsín elected president * 1989: Radicals lose presidential elections; amid growing economic chaos, Alfonsín hands over power to new Peronist President, Carlos Saúl Menem * 1991: start of economic policy with *peso* at parity with US dollar * 1994: new constitution approved, allowing president to serve consecutive terms in office * 1995: Menem wins second term as president.

Constitution: presidential republic. According to reformed 1994 constitution, the president can serve two consecutive terms of four years. Legislative power is exercised by the Congress, which comprises the Senate, with 63 members, and the Chamber of Deputies, which has 261 members, elected for a four-year term. One half of the Chamber of Deputies is renewed every two years. The 23 provinces elect their own governors, and have their own provincial legislatures. Judicial power lies with the Supreme Court and other competent tribunals. The nine Supreme Court judges are chosen by the president with the approval of the Senate.

Head of State: Carlos Saúl Menem (re-elected in May 1995)

Political parties (with seats in Chamber of Deputies and Senate 1996): Partido Justicialista (PJ, Justicialist Party), 132 and 36; Unión Cívica Radical (UCR, Radical party) 71 and 15; Frente del País Solidario (FREPASO, National Solidarity Front) 27 and 2; others 31 and 10.

Military expenditure as % of combined education and health expenditure (1990-91): 51% (UK 40%, US 46%)
Armed forces (1995): army 40,400 (18,100 conscripts); navy 18,000 (3,500 conscripts); airforce 8,900 (1,200 conscripts).
In June 1994 it was announced that Argentina's Army was to be reduced to 23,000 troops during 1995 and that conscription was to be discontinued.
Membership of international organisations: UN and UN organisations, Organisation of American States, G-15, Mercosur customs union (with Brazil, Uruguay and Paraguay).
Media/communications: Argentina has over 200 daily newspapers, most based in provincial cities. There are many weekly magazines and journals and a number of significant book publishers. Approximately 75 private and 35 state-owned radio stations broadcast in different regions, while there are 12 state-owned and 30 independent televison channels, mostly available in the greater Buenos Aires area.

D

ECONOMY

Currency: peso; since April 1991, 1 *peso* = 1 US dollar.
Inflation: 1991: 84%; 1992: 17.7%; 1993: 7.4%; 1994: 3.7%.
Gross Domestic Product (GDP): US$200.3bn (1994)
Per capita GDP (1994): US$6,300

Economic growth: (1990) 0.1%; (1991) 8.9%; (1992) 8.7%; (1993) 6.0; (1994) 6.5%; -2.6% (1995)
Foreign debt: (1990) US$61.0bn; (1991) US$63.7bn; (1992) US$65.0bn; (1993) US$68.0bn; (1994) US$77.5bn; (1995) US$87.5bn.

GDP by sector (1992): services 53.4%; industry 35.9%; agriculture 8.5%; mining 2.3%
Unemployment: (1990) 7.5%; (1991) 6.5%; (1992) 6.9%; (1993) 9.5%; (1994) 11.9%; (1995) 19% (estimate)

Exports and imports and trade balance (billions of US dollars):

	Exports	Imports	Trade Balance
1990	12.4	4.1	8.3
1991	12.0	8.3	3.7
1992	12.2	14.9	-2.7
1993	13.1	16.8	-3.7
1994	15.8	21.6	-5.8

Main exports: cereals, foodstuffs, oils and fats, oil and fuel, fruit and fish.
Main imports: machinery, electrical goods, automobiles, chemicals, iron and steel, plastics.
Principal trading partners (1992):
Imports: Brazil (US$3.3bn); US (US$3.2bn); Germany (US$1.1bn); Italy (US$760m); Japan (US$697m); Chile (US$646m)
Exports: Brazil (US$1.7bn); US (US$1.3bn); Netherlands (US$1.2bn); Germany (US$731m); Chile (US$581m); Italy (US$525)

E ARGENTINA AND BRITAIN/ UNITED STATES

In 1994 Argentine exports to Britain totalled approximately £170m, while British exports to Argentina were valued at £225m. Despite the diplomatic impasse over the question of the Falklands/Malvinas islands' sovereignty, relations, political and economic have improved considerably since 1982.
The US is Argentina's second largest trading partner after Brazil. There is large-scale US investment, with transnationals such as General Motors and IBM operating within Argentina.

ARGENTINA

0   250   500km

◉ Capital (Buenos Aires: 12 m

◉ City with 500,000 - 1 milli

● City with 200,000 - 500,0

● Fewer than 100,000 inhab

⚓ Seaport

✈ International airport

······· Railway

——— Road

——— River

➤ ·· National boundaries

Marsh

Saltmarsh

+ Peak